PN Review 246

VOLUME 45   NUMBER 4   MARCH – APR

REPORTS

POEMS & FEATURES

REVIEWS

Editorial

IN AN AGE THAT INSISTS on transparency in judgement and selection, the back-room of poetry has become a dark place. Accountability is called for, but often the accountants are hidden from sight. Their effects are not recognised as effects, the marks and bruises they leave are powdered and rouged over.

Looking back even twenty years, the culture of reception for poetry was critical. Publishers promoted their writers as best they could, if anything was newsworthy in the work or the life it was magnified and made into a story. But what mattered was the reviewer making the case for or against a new book, engaging with it, arguing, exemplifying. Enough evidence was in a good review for attentive readers to judge for themselves – to judge the judges, as it were. Letters to the editor often contested a disagreeable review (as in the letter that follows this editorial). Dialogue was never far away. Critics might argue with one another, and their arguments engage wider concerns: formal, thematic, political.

Nowadays the political may be at work out of sight, the reader unaware of it. Editors engage with the language of writers, suggesting, retracting, worrying at a work until it is as good as they and the author collaboratively can make. This collaboration is creative. Some editors listen to new writing with a different kind of hearing. One contributor to these pages told us that the editor of a major poetry journal required him to change the word 'deafness' to 'silence' in a poem. The editor was concerned that the use of the word 'deafness' might be considered 'Ablist' by their readers, as though the editor's task was to police the poem on behalf of a sensitised and delicate readership. 'The word "deafness" has great power,' wrote the edited poet, 'there is such a difference between the deaf and the un-listening.' The reader of the published poem will be unaware of the unattested unravelling of texture that has occurred. At least in a palimpsest one can see where erasures have been made.

Another crucial change is that a sometimes accountable, more or less open critical review culture has given way to the prize culture which provides crucial rhetoric for the marketing of books. If an author is shortlisted it becomes part of a permanent record. An author who receives an award can ever after be described as 'award-winning', a title almost as valuable as a knighthood.

Twenty years ago, when critics liked or disliked a book of poems, they had to provide reasons, and they had to reason both with the author and the reader. A review talked over both shoulders, as it were. The complex 'award' process, however, is anything but transparent. I write as someone who has judged national, regional and local competitions. Participation does not lessen the dark room's darkness. First, who chooses the judges, and why are the judges chosen? Can they be chosen in such a way as to affect the likely outcomes of the award-giving process? (They can be, and we must trust that they won't.) And when they make their shortlist, what is their rationale? The process is not asked at that stage to be answerable, the judges' connections within the poetry world are not generally interrogated.

Crucially, the dialogue between judges called upon to consider large swathes of work are not conducted in the open, their arguments are not recorded, and the spin they put on the announcement of their final selections does not include any of what one imagines might, or ought, to be the heat and friction of critical engagement. The final announcement is neutralised, as though a boxing match had occurred offstage and a victor was paraded around the ring wearing a belt no one could quite account for.

Letter to the Editor

ROBYN MARSACK *writes* · Dear Editors, I am writing in belated response to the editorial in *PNR* 243 (Sept–Oct 2018) as an occasional translator and an admirer of Kate Briggs's *This Little Art*. I would not want *PNR* readers to dismiss the book after reading comments that seemed to be based more on Benjamin Moser's review of it in the *NYTBR*, rather than a direct encounter with *This Little Art* itself. It is a pity that this editorial, which obviously wishes to take issue with 'some of the easier rhetorical gestures of contemporary essay-writing' – and may be right to do so – has chosen the responses to *This Little Art* as the vehicle.

First of all, Briggs does not behave like 'a primary artist'. Indeed, her whole 'meditation' – a term to which I'll return – considers the translator's relationship to the original text; it is the crux of the matter. The translator, she suggests, is a 'producer of relations'. (Even the blurb calls translation, as described in the book, 'an intensely relational activity'.) As a translator, her relationship has been principally with Barthes, but also more recently with Zola, and in her book she describes the Dutch translation group she belongs to; there is a faint implication in the criticism that two volumes of Barthes scarcely qualify as a basis for her exploration.

On the very next page from what Moser calls her 'assertion' (not an 'argument', you see) that we are in need of translations, Briggs offers a reason for this need: 'the translations we do read are their own necessary reminder [...] of everything we are not reading, and yet has been written and is being read by so many others' (as she had clearly defined the 'we' as 'the English-speaking world' – why did Moser feel that he had to reduce that to 'middle-class English speakers'?). This is a general argument, it seems to me, and specifying which works we are missing and by whom they should be translated, as Moser demands, is not necessary to it or even particularly useful at this point. Thus we have one motivation for translating: because a work or an author provides something not available to us in English.

Briggs goes on to ask: 'What are the features of this practice of translating?' and thus leads us into an exploration of those features, partly by means of discussing her own experience in translating Barthes in all its material and intellectual distinctiveness. She discusses the work of Helen Loewe Porter and Dorothy Bussy, in particular, but also – as her translator-defenders wrote in their letter to the *NYTBR* – an 'impressively wide range of writers, thinkers and theorists'. Her placing of women translators in their economic, domestic and sentimental contexts was for me a very welcome story of writing/translating lives that I could recognise.

Throughout her essay she refers to the translator as 'she', and I must admit that I found this warming to the same degree, I suspect, as Moser found it – at some level – very irritating. The Editor's conclusion to his opening paragraph is either mischievous or unnecessary in drawing attention to the gender of translators of Camus he simply liked or disliked. He later expresses annoyance at the charge of 'misogynistic sniping' levelled at Moser, so why underline gender differences at the outset of his editorial? I think that this is part of the misunderstanding of Briggs's writing in general, and that it is related to the concept of *écriture feminine*, a concept neither the editor nor Moser might care for, but which seems very useful here: a fluidity of expression that also tends to transgress accepted forms – as does Lispector, at least in the translations by Giovanni Pontiero (which I edited for Carcanet).

The Editor suggests that Briggs's 'lyrical essay mode lets her off a range of scholarly and critical responsibilities... it would seem that she was writing poetry, or a sonata, or creating a collage', he writes, 'but not a critical meditation'. (Why shouldn't an essay take sonata form, though? Exposition, development and recapitulation do not seem inimical to critical responsibilities.) He and Moser suggest that her way of writing cannot answer to the demands – as they conceive them – of the essay form. I think differently. It is the form of this meditation that is innovative, illuminating and thought provoking. It is a form that gives us insight into the *process* of thinking about and making a translation. The requirement to be 'critical' is less obvious than the requirement to be intelligently discriminating about the experience of reading and writing translations, which Briggs simply is.

She understands the importance of the pleasure taken by the translator in the original text as key to motivation, and as accounting for 'what otherwise looks like the strikingly haphazard history of literature in translation: a factor, along with all the other powerful and determining forces of economics, status, chance and circumstance, that works to determine what gets translated, and when, and by whom'. And – speaking of responsibilities: 'To be clear: it is not my intention to downplay the knowledge that is involved in translating', but – asking the critical question: 'Tell me, really: when could anyone, any reader or writer, consider themselves adequately *pre*-qualified to undertake the translation of, say, a 730-page novel set in a sanatorium? One of Germany's most formative contributions to European literature?' Her answer is that translators undertake their work not to demonstrate their expertise 'but precisely because they know, without yet knowing exactly how or in what particular ways, doing so will be productive of *new* knowledge', of the world and of writing.

Moser's tone and his aim were directed towards a book he profoundly misunderstood. *This Little Art* is, I believe, intended as a conversation: the author with herself as she constantly questions her own practice and assumptions; and the conversation she opens up with her readers, inviting them to consider the texts and ideas she lays side by side, developing or even discarding them as she goes along. It is an intelligent, open book, and perhaps that very openness was what disconcerted Moser, and could not be appreciated by someone who has not read it from cover to cover. I urge readers of *PNR*, a publication which has brought us many and varied translations, to read *This Little Art* with the attention it merits.

Cover Story

Marc Atkins, 'Orfordness'

MARC ATKINS is best known for his photographs of urban space, especially of London. But he has created an equally large number of landscape studies. As with the cityscapes, the environment in these images has been shaped twice over – once by the cumulative history of its use, and then by the artist's response based on his reading of that use. In this image, the marshy foreground is supplied by Orford Ness, while the ghostly structure in the background has been transplanted from elsewhere. This spectral architecture is hauntingly beautiful but it also resembles a stylised mushroom cloud, looming over a vulnerable ecosystem used for over seventy years as a key site for military experimentation, including the testing of nuclear weapons. In all of Atkins's photographic works, a mysterious intensity is achieved by subjecting the visible terrain to the pressure of an artistic vision. Few artists in any medium have rendered a critique of land use as powerfully and palpably as Atkins does with his camera.

ROD MENGHAM

News & Notes

A Poet's Reading · John Ashbery's personal library of some five thousand volumes 'will now be getting space on the shelves at Harvard University, his alma mater', Jennifer Schuessler wrote in the *New York Times*. Harvard's Houghton Library began acquiring the poet's manuscripts and other papers in 1986. His 'reading library' includes poetry, art criticism, architectural history, philosophy, religious history and cookbooks. The collection was donated by David Kermani, Ashbery's long-time partner, and includes annotated editions of books by Pasternak, Kafka, Nietzsche and many others. His undergraduate *Oxford Book of American Verse* contains pressed flowers used as bookmarks.

A New Divan: A Lyrical Dialogue between East & West · In late May 2019, Gingko will publish *A New Divan* to celebrate the 200th anniversary of the first publication of Goethe's great poem sequence the *West-Eastern Divan*, which was inspired by his reading of Joseph von Hammer's 1814 translation of the poems of the fourteenth-century Persian poet Hafiz and by his love affair with Marianne von Willemer, 'Suleika' to his 'Hatem'. Gingko facilitates dialogue between the Middle East and the Western world through conferences, events and scholarly publications. Its aim is to enable constructive, informed and open discussion, giving a voice to a new generation of thinkers and opinion formers. *A New Divan* extends this conversation into the realm of poetry.

   A New Divan is an anthology of two dozen original poems – twelve by poets from the 'East' (including Adonis, Abbas Beydoun, Mohammed Bennis and Fatemeh Shams) and a dozen from the 'West' (including Homero Aridjis, Raoul Schrott, Angélica Freitas and Clara Janés). Each poem appears in *A New Divan* in a translation by a leading English-language poet facing the original language of composition. Among these poets are Bill Manhire, Sinéad Morrissey, Lavinia Greenlaw, Robin Robertson and Jo Shapcott. The poems by Abbas Beydoun and Mohammed Bennis in English versions by Bill Manhire and Sinéad Morrissey will appear in *PN Review* 247.

Prizes · Simon Armitage was awarded the Queen's gold medal for poetry 2018. Carol Ann Duffy in her citation made him sound like a social worker, a political activist and a missionary: his poems 'would challenge hypocrisy wherever they encountered it, giving voice to those rarely admitted into poetry, and extending an arm around the unheard and the dispossessed. And for all the attention to the grain and trouble of daily lives, the poems never lost sight of wider horizons: our outer space full of possibilities, the dream space of our love.' The poems may do some or all of those things, but they do a great deal more *as* poems. · The Bollingen Prize, administered through the Beinecke Rare Book and Manuscript Library at Yale, is awarded every two years to recognise a recent book or a lifetime body of work. In choosing Charles Bernstein as the fifty-first winner, this year's judges – Ange Mlinko, Claudia Rankine and Evie Shockley – said that throughout his career Bernstein 'has shaped and questioned, defined and dismantled ideas and assumptions in order to reveal poetry's widest and most profound capabilities.' · The Arts Foundation Future Awards announced that Will Harris has won the £10,000 Poetry Fellowship supported by the David Collins Foundation. Tracey Emin presented the award. Previous winners include Alice Oswald (1993), Ahren Warner (2012) and Hollie McNish (2015). Judge Sarah Howe declared, 'You would struggle to find a keener mind at work in the form than his, and yet these poems are as loving as they are contemplative, passionate in their political commitments.'

Hydra · *Bruce Harris* writes: Alan Morrison's seventh poetry collection *Shadows Waltz Haltingly* (Lapwing Publications, 2015) referred to his mother's illness and subsequent death from the genetic illness Huntington's Disease. My partner of over thirty years, Anthony, was diagnosed with HD in October 2016, and from that time onwards, all my takings from my published books have been donated to Huntington's Disease charities. Alan had already published my work in his magazine *The Recusant*. When I began to write about HD as it related to Anthony and me, Alan's help with forming the poems into a new collection for his Caparison imprint was a relief and an inspiration. *The Huntington Hydra*, likening HD to the legendary monster, is mostly about life before, during and after diagnosis. Anthony and I agreed to aim at raising both funds and awareness. The book contains a foreword from the Huntington's Disease Association. Poetry with as direct a purpose as this remains rare, though many poets past and present confront the serious experiences of their lives through writing. Huntington's Disease is still incurable, despite promising research developments. It has transformed and intensified our lives. (*The Huntington Hydra*, www.therecusant.org.uk)

Desnos · *Karl O'Hanlon* writes: 'The re-publication of Martin Bell's Robert Desnos translations, edited by his muse Christine McCausland, with my foreword, has been published privately.' It is a handsome book, a snip at £9.99, and available from Art Translated, 31 St Mary's Terrace, Hastings, TN3 3LR, UK.

Bookish Rock Star · Mary Oliver, who won a Pulitzer Prize, was widely read and loved, but divided critics, has died at the age of eighty-three. She published more than a score of poetry books and won a National Book Award in 1992 for *New and Selected Poems*. She equalled Billy Collins in some of her book sales. Her poems use plain language and accessible references and are generally brief. They teach lessons and are for the most part – as the ministers who used her work in sermons might have said – uplifting. Her poetry readings were spectacularly well-attended. 'Fairly late in life', the *Times* obituarist suggested, she developed 'the aura of a reluctant, bookish rock star'. She said her vocation was 'the observation of life'. She seems to come quite close to the reader, an almost intimate proximity, and it can be hard not to assent to her spell. Her appeal was not universal. David Orr in the *New York Times* described her as a writer 'about whose poetry one can only say that no animals appear to have been harmed in the making of it'. Taking another approach, Alicia Gregory declared, 'Her corpus is deceptively elementary...' Her love of Edna St Vincent Millay's work, and her debts to her, are very much to her credit. In 'When Death Comes' she wrote: 'When it's over, I want to say: all my life / I was a bride married to amazement.'

Silence in China · *Ed Hsu* writes: Meng Lang, an exiled Chinese poet, died of lung cancer on 12 December 2018 at the age of fifty-seven. Tributes were published across the media, with memorial events in Hong Kong and Taipei. In the 1980s, Meng Lang became active in the underground poetry scene in China. At this time, he co-edited and published an anthology of Chinese underground poetry, promoting banned poets' works. His English translator Denis Mair describes his life 'like a migratory bird's'. He left China in 1995 for Brown University, Providence, Rhode Island, as a visiting poet. He began his life in exile, living between the United States and Hong Kong. In the early 2000s, he met his Taiwanese wife in Hong Kong and later moved and lived there. Shortly after 2010, freedom of speech was under threat in Hong Kong. Meng and his wife moved to Hualien in Taiwan in 2015. In early 2018, whilst in Hong Kong launching a poetry collection to commemorate the Chinese political dissident Liu Xiaobo, Meng's health deteriorated. Following news of his illness, the 'Save Meng Lang' fundraising campaign was launched to help with the cost of his treatments in Hong Kong.

Described by the *New York Times* as the 'poet who promoted dissident writers', Meng Lang was uncompromising in his efforts against repressive power. He co-founded the Independent Chinese PEN Centre in 2001 to promote freedom of expression and publication for writers in the Chinese language. He was a long-time supporter of the Nobel Peace Prize Laureate, the fellow poet Liu Xiaobo. Meng with other supporters campaigned for Liu's prison release to go abroad for medical treatments.

Meng's poetry unflinchingly depicts the world, using both realism and surrealism. His language can be exquisite and experimental. Readers experience the pain and despair at its root. The lighter poems offer a more spirited reading experience. As he wrote, in Denis Mair's translation:

> Silence in China, being openly published
> Openly propagandizing, openly agitating
> Its ten thousand pairs, yes ten thousand pairs of pure wings.

Meng Lang will be remembered as a political activist. His poetry of resistance will continue to spread its anger and hope.

Hellfast · *Siobhan Campbell* writes: Poet Padraic Fiacc has died in Belfast (21 Jan). Born there as Patrick Joseph O'Connor in 1924, he emigrated as a child with his family to Hell's Kitchen, New York City. Educated in Commerce and Haaren high schools, Manhattan, he once studied for the priesthood. A four-year sojourn in 1946 was followed by a permanent return to Belfast (which he sometimes terms 'Hellfast') in 1956. From the poems, we know that Fiacc struggled with the advice of his first mentor Padraic Colum, who encouraged him to write of subjects beloved of the Irish Revival. He worked to find an aesthetic to match his sense of profound dislocation and unease, coupled with a sense of poet as a kind of 'witness'. With his first collection *Woe to the Boy* published in 1957 and five more before *Semper Vacare* (1999), it's possible to trace a poetic development that experimented with ways of allowing political and cultural struggles into the poem. Making aesthetic decisions stimulated by moral feeling, he wrote poems to mirror the chronic instability of his social arena in ways which suggest that this destabilised the poem itself, the line, and even the word. A forthcoming article in this magazine will expand on this reading of the work.

Romantic Legacies · *Ian Pople* writes: Michael O'Neill, who died on 21 December 2018 at the age of sixty-five, was an authoritative commentator on Romanticism, in particular the work of Shelley, on whom he published his first two academic books. In addition, he edited, with Zachary Leader, the OUP edition of Shelley's major works. O'Neill also wrote on Yeats, the 1930s poets and Dante. His study *The All-Sustaining Air* examined the legacies of Romanticism in the work of a range of twentieth-century poets from Yeats and Eliot, to Paul Muldoon, Geoffrey Hill and Roy Fisher. He himself was an award-winning poet. The recipient of a Gregory Award in 1983, he published his first collection, *The Stripped Bed*, with Collins Harvill in 1990. This book won a Cholmondeley Award. Michael's poetry was wise and empathetic. In person, he was generous, gracious and possessed a quiet charisma. His dedication to his students was repaid with a full house at Durham University for the launch of *Return of the Gift*, and he was doing PhD supervisions in the last week of his life. A final volume of poetry, *Crash and Burn*, is due from Arc in April of this year.

Sundry Identities · Poet, essayist, playwright and polemicist Tom Leonard died in December aged seventy-four. In 2001, along with friends and fellow writers Alasdair Gray and James Kelman, he was appointed Joint Professor of Creative Writing at Glasgow University, a post he held till retirement in 2009. One obituary described him as 'a fierce intelligence sliced through with a strong moral vein'. He was hostile to the hegemony of Standard English and keen on poetry in live performance. 'All livin' language is sacred', he said. He contributed to *PN Review* between 1994 and 2008, his last original contribution being the short poem 'Odysseus':

> it took me so long to get back to who I am
> why was I away so long why was the journey so tortuous
> all those false masks against a backdrop narrative to do with
>   authenticity
>
> but now arriving back there is still much debris to clear
> the clearer to see the point from which I started
>
> that from which I set out confused in sundry identities at war
>   with themselves
> now to find calm on that setting-out point as the final desti-
>   nation

Letter from Trinidad

Of Snakes and Stiltwalkers

Vahni Capildeo

The driveway sloped down to the west-facing boundary of the house, a half-height, green-painted brick wall inset with a row of black-painted metal railings. These railings were thick with bougainvillea. Along the lower part of the wall, the wanted and unwanted shrubs and vines were trimmed to a common height, but too mixed up for the eye to disentangle stem from vine or leaves from brickwork. The electric gate stood between two pillars at the end of the driveway. It had begun to malfunction. It opened and closed at random. Sometimes one side approaching quicker than the other was triggered by the other side into flying open again. Sometimes both sides closed, slowly, but stopped just before they shut tight.

The men who were mending the electric gate had found a snake. There are rare reptiles on the island. Ideally an expert is called, and the thing is rescued. There are poisonous reptiles on the island, including the fer-de-lance, one of the few snakes anywhere that will turn and charge an intruder on its territory, rather than slinking away. The men were keen to do their job well. They called the lady of the house to see the snake. What did the senior lady of the house say? 'Kill it quickly,' perhaps? 'Please deal with it'? In any case, she felt the kind of terror and extreme disgust that are inseparable from each other. She may not have said anything. She passed as quickly as she could, on her nerve-damaged legs, into the house. Somehow, she communicated the presence of the snake, and the need to do something, to the people in the household. I was there, and I went out.

The men, feeling a little deserted, had come with shy machismo part way up the driveway. They did not cross the invisible threshold that separated the doorless garage from the garden space. The younger one had a machete. His elbow was low, and his hand was high. The machete pointed downwards. The snake was impaled on it. The astonishingly bright green-gold body moved in mid-air. It described pain. 'You need to kill it,' I said. The snake was flipped off. Feeling the ground beneath its belly, it began to move with more confidence. The man cut it in half. It described an arc of pain. 'No, you need to crush its head,' I said. I spoke kindly and quietly, because he was keen to do its job well. 'The part where the head joins the neck. Otherwise it's still alive.' Theatrically, he lifted his boot. He stamped. A royal red spurt under his heel left jelly on the garage floor. That would need cleaned. Suddenly sure of what to do, the men took the body out to the grass verge beyond the gate. They would leave it there for the birds; the green-gold colour dulled fast. In that way, at the back of the house, we leave overripe fruit for the birds. They clean it.

Although their ideas were not mine, I recognised that the repair men had a code of behaviour for how to do a job well. What extras the job might entail (reporting and disposing of snakes, for example) was part of keeping the boundary safe. Gatekeeping: this must be why they had parked their truck as if blockading the driveway, while working on the motor. My desire to preserve a variety of life, or to avoid cruelty or mess, might have made sense to them; but why? What I wanted, if I knew what to do, had not been intelligible, not in the way I communicated it. Neither of us had the knowledge to decode the other: priorities, housekeeping, risk-taking, tone of voice, body language... oh it can be so bare, trying to go by words. Not being forward, not being aggressive, not acting on their own interpretation without an explicit command, may have been part of their code. Being deferential can be a transgenerational survivor habit. So can having zero expectations of the well-housed employer's preferences, kindness, logic, common sense, or basic sanity. I recognised a craft in the use of the machete. That craft could have been, at other times probably was, deployed in manifold ways, mostly unimaginable to me; I knew only of the most basic – breaking ground, pruning trees, delicately slicing spoon-like implements from a green coconut shell.

The webs of relation in which I found myself in Trinidad, the proximity to differing crafts, reminded me of Nisha Ramayya's proposal of a 'Tantric poetics' in Sandeep Parmar, Nisha Ramayya and Bhanu Kapil's *Threads* (clinic, 2018). She takes 'Tantra' ('etymologically cognate with "text"') back and forth from its meanings to do with patterning, with being both 'frame' and 'threads'. The following quotation is not a simple representation of her proposal, which is far-reaching and complex. It is a sample of the revolutionary, precise weaving and unweaving by which Ramayya's thought processes evolve the proposal as if co-thinking with the reader:

> A Tantric poetics affirms closeness, relationship and community, without enforcing touch, agreement, or commonality. A Tantric poetics realises the possibilities of relating without sharing interests, without getting on, without liking – we can dislike each other without denying each other's possibilities.

As I write this, I am in seated in the economy class aisle seat of the second aeroplane of my day, 35,000 feet above the Indian Ocean. The holy man in saffron robes who was sitting in the middle seat when I arrived has moved to the window seat, so as not to sit next to a potentially impure being. I heard him use the word 'lady' as he explained his seat swap to the man who is now asleep between us, the blue cap pulled over his eyes not really shading him from anything except the feeling of exposure to sleeping among strangers. I cannot decode the less-holy man's religion – so many in the region are a little similar – but from the signs and tokens and rituals familiar to my Hindu diaspora upbringing in Port of Spain, I can tell that the thread circling his right wrist is not an ornament, but a talisman.

The sea keeps me thinking of Trinidad: of Moko Jumbies, the stiltwalkers, euphoric on their two-foot, four-foot, six-foot, nine, twelve, fifteen-foot stilts, who channel the vengeful, healing West African god. He crossed the Atlantic, walking behind the slave ships. Not so long ago, he/they walked back, for a performance and installation in London. Who is looking and listening, I wonder? Who will be for the healing and who for the vengeance? Who will take plenty falls until they 'touch the sky'? I reopen *Threads*, balanced on my lap. I think about the gravity and dizziness of a poetics of vectors and points, at each of which the reader takes a sounding of an ever-changing relation to different currents and crafts.

Peter Porter and Music

William Poulos

Like a kookaburra's laugh, Peter Porter's poetry is musical but not entirely euphonic. Even in his 'mature' poetry we find lines such as, 'Then, beside the church where a clapped-out pigeon fell / to be picked up by a not-very-poor-looking Italian – was...' and 'open the dictionary of discontinuity'. One can barely say these lines, but they were written by a poet who collaborated with many composers and said that the poet should prioritise sound over meaning, 'follow[ing] the tread of language rather than the thread of thought'. Porter's moderated mellifluousness was evident early. I only had to read the last stanza from 'Who Gets the Pope's Nose?' once before it was permanently in my head:

> And high above Rome in a room with a wireless
> The Pope also waits to die.
> God is the heat in July
> And the iron band of pus tightening in the chest.
> Of all God's miracles, death is the greatest.

One of the best things about this stanza is the full stop after 'die' which is as affecting as a rest in a melody. Recognising, however, that music's power comes from a combination of consonance and dissonance, Porter, even at his most lyrical, was often raucous. This makes him a more musical poet than, say, Tennyson. His models were composers; he often spoke admiringly of Bach and Schubert, who wrote so much yet strained so little, and his volume of output and speed of composition were attempts to imitate them. He thought that music was *the* transcendental art. In *Three Poems for Music* he wrote: 'And Paradise, till we are there / is in these measured lengths of air.' Music brings us closer to God than even Shakespeare's language does. In his essay *The Shape of Poetry and the Shape of Music*, Porter mentions a scene in *Anthony and Cleopatra* in which a soldier talks to a companion before Anthony's last and ruinous battle. The soldier says ''tis the god Hercules whom Anthony loved, now leaves him' and the stage direction reads 'hautboys beneath'. Porter doesn't really care what the music was, but its presence notes an important part of the play: 'the gods speak to us ambiguously... and for their deepest impartings, they use music, the supreme oracle.'

Porter imitates musical consonance and dissonance to transcend the physical world in his poem 'An Exequy', written after his first wife killed herself in the attic. He prepares to join her in death and octosyllabics describe her ghost leading him to the afterlife:

> Then take my hand and lead me out,
> The sky is overcast by doubt,
> The time has come, I listen for
> Your words of comfort at the door,
> O guide me through the shoals of fear –
> 'Fürchte dich nicht, ich bin bei dir.'

Ending such a lyrical poem with a line in German stymies and infuriates some readers, especially the critics who rebuke Porter for what they call his pointless displays of erudition. The last line is vexing but not pointless. For a start, it's a good way of expressing the shock of death (an earlier line says 'the hand is stopped upon the clock') and the horrid climax Porter finds at the top of the stairs. The line harmonises with the rest of the poem in metre, rhyme and meaning; it's the first line of Bach's Motet BWV 228, which was probably written for a funeral. Furthermore, it's a translation of Isaiah 43:10: 'Fear not, for I am with you'. The full verse, as rendered by King James's translators, reads: 'Fear thou not; for I am with thee: be not dismayed; for I am thy God: I will strengthen thee; yea, I will help thee; yea, I will uphold thee with the right hand of my righteousness.' Combining dissonance and an allusion to music, the last line of 'An Exequy' conveys Porter's transcendental movement.

Yet for Porter music transcends even God. The last collection he released while alive was called *Better than God*, and the title poem can usefully be quoted in full:

> As He said of the orchestra
> at the Creation, they can play
> anything you put in front of them.

Porter's compression doesn't reveal exactly *what* is better than God. I suspect it's the human creation of music which supersedes God's creation. But I'm basing this on remarks in Porter's other works, such as a couplet from *Three Poems to Music* which says that 'virtuosi of the earth / outsang the Gods who gave them birth', and a remark in *The Shape of Poetry and the Shape of Music*: 'In Eden we were all listeners, but what we heard were the unimprovable sounds of Nature. Since the expulsion, we have made much more beautiful and complex sounds for ourselves. And called them poetry and music.' This suggests to me that Porter tried to capture the complexity of music rather than the simplicity of tunes.

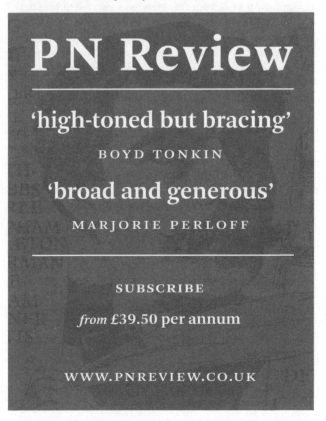

Letter from Wales

SAM ADAMS

My previous 'letter' was accompanied by a photograph of three important figures in the cultural life of Wales in the twentieth century, the artist Kyffin Williams and two writers, R. S. Thomas and Emyr Humphreys, for both of whom Welsh was a second language largely learned in adulthood. Welsh became their preferred medium of oral communication and both wrote and published work in Welsh, but the creative writing that made and sustains their reputations is in English. A good many contemporary Welsh writers in English have taken a similar journey towards bilingualism as adults, inspired by their late realisation of the long history in these islands and cultural value of Welsh.

There are again those few, who, like Gwyneth Lewis, are thoroughly and creatively bilingual from the outset, and also the unusual cases of writers who, having learned Welsh, choose to engage with the language at the more intense and demanding level of creative expression. It is not a decision to be taken lightly. Conrad thought it demanded 'a fearful effort'. Meic Stephens, who learned Welsh after taking a degree in French at UCW Aberystwyth, was the ideal obituarist when Robert Maynard Jones died in November 2017, for Bobi Jones, the name by which he became known as a writer, had also learned Welsh, beginning at grammar school in Cardiff where the usual curricular limitations meant pupils studied either French or Welsh. He would say later that he didn't choose the subject, it chose him. An outstanding student career at UC Cardiff and in Dublin in due course took him to the chair of Welsh language and literature at UCW Aberystwyth, a post he held from 1980 until retirement. His enormous contribution to Welsh culture includes co-founding Yr Academi Gymreig in 1957 (with his friend Waldo Williams) and, inspired by his own experience as a Welsh learner, Cymdeithas y Dysgwyr (the Welsh Learners Society). Alongside academic work ranging widely from the middle ages to contemporary literature, he kept up an extraordinary output of poetry, novels, short stories and critical studies – in all, over a hundred books in Welsh. His belief in Christianity was as profound and vivid as his commitment to poetry: in 1958 he wrote, 'Angau, 'rwyt ti'n fy ofni i / Am fy mod yn fardd' ('Death you fear me / for I am a poet').

In 2012, Meic Stephens published his Hunangofiant (autobiography) in Welsh (though there is an English version, My Shoulder to the Wheel, also from Y Lolfa, 2015). He regularly competed for the Crown at the National Eisteddfod with long poem sequences, often in Gwenhwyseg, the south-east Wales dialect of Welsh, missing the prize by a whisker on several occasions. For many, his crowning achievement was the Oxford Companion to the Literature of Wales (1986), but it may not be as widely recognised that in parallel with the OUP production he also edited Cydymaith i Lenyddiaeth Cymru, the Welsh language version, which was published by the University of Wales Press in the same year. His assistant on the latter was Christine James, from Tonypandy, who learned Welsh at a Rhondda grammar school, graduated in Welsh at Aberystwyth and was awarded a doctorate for work on

the laws of Hywel Dda. Recently retired as professor of Welsh at Swansea University, she is also a poet of distinction. She won the Crown at the National Eisteddfod in 2005 and the Wales Book of the Year prize for poetry in Welsh in 2014 with Rhwng y Llinellau ('Between the Lines'). She became the first woman Archdruid of Wales, presiding over National Eisteddfod ceremonies from 2013 to 2016, and currently she is the first woman to serve as Cofiadur (Recorder) of the Eisteddfod's Gorsedd of Bards.

A lecture at the National Museum in Cardiff gave a taste of Professor James's current interests. She is researching popular images of the Welsh as revealed in broadside ballads now preserved in collections at the University of California (the EBBA website) and the Bodleian Library. The best known, as familiar as nursery rhyme, 'Taffy was a Welshman, Taffy was a thief', has an ignominiously long history. As late as the 1890s it was a convenient paradigm for opponents of disestablishment of the Anglican church:

> Taffy scoffs at English, and prefers his native bards,
> Who splutter Cambrian gibberish at Eisteddfods by yards;
> They twingle-twangle creaky harps, they munch their leeks
>   and cheese,
> Hymning to hillside goats their bosom friends the Cymric
>   fleas.

This late and venomously hostile piece aimed at the Welsh in general includes markers familiar to students of the genre. 'Splutter' is taken from a 'Welsh' oath that appears repeatedly in ballads from the seventeenth century and probably earlier, 'od splutter hur nails', which originally was meant to stand for a Welsh mangling of 'God's blood and nails', though this is not recognised by some commentators. It is an expression used by the Welsh giant even in recent re-tellings of the tale of 'Jack the Giant Killer'. The 'hur', which occurs whenever a Welshman speaks in a ballad, could be put down to an English failure to hear clearly, or listen attentively, but Professor James points out that the Welsh personal pronoun 'hi', meaning both 'she' and 'her', and pronounced 'he' is a potential source of confusion that may colour aural perception, especially since it is also used to form the possessive. Whatever the source of this curiosity, it had strong powers of adhesion. 'The Welshman's Praise of Wales' from 1700 ends thus:

> Hur has not been in England long,
> And canno speak the Englis Tongue;
> Put hur is hur Friend, and so hur will prove,
> Pray send hur word, if hur can love.

At the nub of it all is the unyielding problem of a different language, 'Cambrian gibberish', deemed impenetrable and, sadly, for most not worth the trouble of trying to understand.

As ubiquitous as 'hur' is the association of the Welsh in balladry with leeks, cheese and goats. 'The Welch Wedding betwixt Ap-Shinkin and Shinny' (1671–1704) is illustrated with a woodcut, in this case representing the bridegroom presumably, though it seems to have been re-used countless times in different contexts. He is a soldier, a pikeman with weapon over his shoulder and sheathed long dagger at his waist. A leek, his badge, is secured by the band of his tall-crowned hat and as shield he bears before him on the end of his knife a round of roast cheese on toast. In the background is a tumbling stream and, beyond, mountains where goats are grazing. Another, cruder, version has Shinkin marching off, pike on shoulder, sword at his side. There is something almost affectionate about these depictions that seems to date from an earlier time, the time perhaps when Shakespeare could create in Fluellen a character eccentric, odd in speech, but worthy, honourable and brave. The goats and the cheese and leeks of the ballads became markers of Welsh peasant poverty and ignorance at a time when the great majority of the English were peasants, equally impoverished and ignorant, though of course there was always the language problem. A brief 'Song to the Old Britons, on St Taffy's Day' (to be sung to the tune 'Of Noble Race Was Shinkin') of about 1715, suggests another reason for the implied gloating superiority of ballad writers:

> How are the Mighty fallen!
> Is this the Brave, the Haughty!
> Highflown Taff, that us'd to quaff
> And bear his Head so lofty!
> Fa, la, la, lara, & c

The Tudor period had brought the Welsh to prominence in England. Are we seeing in broadsheet ballads an expression of deep-seated English resentment of the Welsh that didn't fade with the passage of time but, encouraged by the popular form (they were all meant to be sung), continued, becoming scoffing or vitriolic as occasion demanded?

---

from The Notebooks of Arcangelo Riffis

MARIUS KOCIEJOWSKI

I wish we had spoken of a film I knew Arcangelo grudgingly admired, based on a play by Tennessee Williams, a writer who, for the most part, he greatly disliked. I think one reason we never spoke of *Night of the Iguana* was because he found it impossible to square what he perceived of as truly good with a despised source. A good poem by a poet he loathed, Auden, for example, was allowed no admittance, likewise a piece of music, say Benjamin Britten, for whom he had a special hatred. There are references to *Night of the Iguana* in the notebooks that would seem to suggest the film stumped him. There is a scene in it that should have spoken to him loud and clear. The virginal Hannah Jelkes character describes a mildly perverse act, although it was strong stuff for the time, which she forgives in the one who committed it. 'Nothing human disgusts me, Mr Shannon,' she says, 'unless it's unkind, violent.' It is as moving a scene as any I have seen on screen and I think one of the reasons it works as it does is because, as played by Deborah Kerr, Hannah Jelkes tells it without so much a falter in her voice. As I read Arcangelo's childhood tale, her words kept coming back to me.

Why did we argue so much? Why did I endure him for another three decades or more? It's what people ask me and I say yes, but. *But what?* And then I have a mental struggle of sorts, any resolution to which makes no sense to anyone else much less me. Solve that riddle and my work will be done. I shall set my book against his gravestone. So many friendships are inexplicable, and indeed the inexplicable may be at their root, as if at certain points in our lives we require incompatibility as a measure to what we like to call our tolerance. Were there ever two people more destined to collide? We might have set out from opposite ends of the universe and still the chances of our not meeting in Earls Court would have been infinitesimally remote. Collide we most certainly did and Arcangelo's notebooks of the time display a spleen such as he never expresses toward anyone else in over five thousand pages. I was to occasion the only instance in them where he resorts to obscene language. It was as if his hatred of what the world had become found its object in a single creature, me, and for my part I was quite prepared to give him the worst of myself because the worst is what he brought out in me. My aim was sure, and, summoning the forces of *flib* and *flob*, I'd send him off on another diatribe. Jesus, I was good. I really was. I had him quivering sometimes. Arcangelo's aim was sure as well in that I couldn't defend my own specious arguments and so, spotting the weaknesses, he'd crack the whip to his horses and run his chariot over me. Admittedly, I was a sore loser and I'd splutter with righteous rage but when it came to sending another man over the edge I gave him more than he bargained for and more often than not I did so against my own cherished principles. And so he tarred me with the same brush that he tarred all of existence. A man wiser to me would not have made that mistake. A man wiser to himself might have reached the conclusion that I was in the same boat as he was, unmoored, struggling to find a voice in a world in which our old voices could no longer operate. We were both, although for quite different reasons, lost to ourselves.

I was intolerant of his intolerance. My sighting of John Betjeman on Earls Court Road came early into our talk. Although I was never a great admirer of his verses, they being a species of Englishness as inexplicable as marmite, I had nothing against them either. I thought their author an amiable, talented buffoon who now and then struck a serious note. Arcangelo loathed him. As he always did with people he disliked he distorted his name, on this occasion into something that was an echo of *pyjamas* but not quite. It might have been 'Pyjaman'. Why, though, rough over a buffoon? What harm did he ever do anyone, except, perhaps, to diminish his or her critical faculties? Also I liked people who liked Betjeman. And Betjeman probably liked the people I liked. And he'd done his bit for the preservation of English churches, hadn't he? Arcangelo's habit of mocking people by contorting their names greatly annoyed me. I told him they were sacrosanct and not to be trifled with and that indeed one could make merry with the name *he* was born with. I will not say here what it is or *was*. I will grant him what surely he would grant me. Arcangelo ignored me, however, and continued to call Auden 'Ordure' and Auden's composer friend 'Benjie Brittle' and so on and so on and when in the notebooks he does call them by their proper names he refuses to capitalise them because in his mind they are not deemed worthy of the upper case.

Where we really clashed, though, was with respect to my enthusiasms of the time, which admittedly were youthful and often exploratory in nature and which I'd go so far as to say were necessary steps in the formation of my own artistic identity in that they had to include elements of the mistaken that could be righted only by me. It's what's called learning the hard way. It's what some people called 'processing' although the word so used bugs me. Obstacles are what I've always put before me. I jump them one by one. It takes time. My enthusiasms included almost everything he loathed from Samuel Beckett ('Bucket'), who at the time morbidly fascinated me, to the films of Jacques Rivette (in particular a favourite of mine, *Céline and Julie Go Boating*), to Ted Hughes whose *Crow*, a negative deity, was my constant companion, to the blue paintings of Yves Klein that were then recently at the Tate, to a Québécois friend of mine, Pierre Hamelin, who painted massive canvases of small differently coloured hexagons, which, like Mark Rothko's paintings, had a most peculiar, though indefinable and calming, effect on me. This last, although Arcangelo had never seen any of the work, particularly got his ire and the more tiresome he became on the matter the more entrenched I became, such that I was prepared to defend those hexagons to the death, even at the expense of the whole of the Western tradition of painting. Ye gods, I was ready to commit even his beloved Titian to the skip. When so challenged, my perversity knew no bounds. Spleen, then, gallons of it, and what splenetic notebooks they are that chronicle the beginnings of our relationship. I can barely stomach them. 'I have a knack for always being on the wrong (i.e. untrendy, socially inexpedient) side of the fence,' he writes. There is, however, a vital difference between being put there and putting oneself there. A fixed position allows for only one view of the universe and it was this he raised to a high principle.

All came to a head at Christmas 1974 when Arcangelo presented my girlfriend with a copy of Arianna Stassinopoulos's *The Female Woman*, clearly intended as a guide to how women of her supposedly feministic tendencies ought to behave. Arcangelo in his attitude towards woman was not so much Neanderthal as something that came some millions of years before hirsute men dragged women by their beehives to their caves. Her first reaction upon opening the present was to burst into tears because, after all, what woman wants to be told she is wanting in womanhood; her second was to write him an angry letter. 'I am an oaf & a lummox,' Arcangelo wrote upon receiving it. A month later, he confesses: 'I am dismal company these days. I've been obsessed to the point of mania by trying to make natural sense out of distempered trivia & unnatural disorder without compromising & blurring those essential values & spiritual absolutes without which life makes no sense whatsoever.' Yet no apology was made. A little later he describes himself as feeling like 'a bronze age Mycenaean warrior stranded among Byzantine eunuchs.'

And what was I? I shudder at the pages he devoted to me. I was 'a pathetic stir-crazy relic of Kounter-Kulchur &

Flower Power adulterated & corrupted by later noxious & bent fads & trends... so irredeemably phoney that any attempt to argue with him is like trying to nail jelly against a wall.' Furthermore, I occupied 'a bloodless, gutless dimension of catchphrases, platitudes & adulterated truisms, where anything can mean nothing & nothing can mean anything at all.' Good lines, would that they were aimed at the right face. 'A crazy jigsaw puzzle with many pieces missing': that's what I was. There are many pages in which he goes on in this vein and at one point he speaks of 'pummelling bloody a scribbler' (me) 'who pronounced Vernon Watkins a bad poet.' There I really was to blame. I'd attacked a poet who Arcangelo had thrust upon me, and whose excellence I would come to recognise only much later. I'd done so in order to get at the man who had dismissed all my enthusiasms or, at best, looked condescendingly upon them. Then he accuses me in his journals of not having read Shakespeare and even, dear heavens, D. H. Lawrence: apparently I had argued in favour of the latter without having read a single novel or poem by him. Arcangelo accused Lawrence of always whispering in the reader's ear, which is a fair enough judgment, but was this sufficient to dismiss the whole of his oeuvre? [...]

Seemingly I was not alone. Arcangelo writes: 'It took the alienation of the chaste affections of a lady a year ago to jar me into full realisation of the deterioration my social character had undergone over five years. The jagged & torturous nature that my social intercourse with men had assumed over the same period might have brought me to this awareness sooner. Acquaintances with several men began with geniality & conviviality, and often deep conversation, but gradually went off because a snarling of wavelengths or instances of tactlessness on their part, and ending with my clamming up & freezing them out of my life.' Such admissions might have indicated self-criticism, but there was to be no such enlightenment for no sooner does he write this than he concludes: 'I feel no self-reproach whatsoever. It's been bad politics but that's not my game anyway. In every instance my snap evaluation of the fellow's character proved to be right & my dislike justified even when not in the least apparent at first. I could never assume or maintain a false position among men even out of kindness or good manners.' If, as he said of me, there were no channels of confluence, only points of static and abrasion, then it was because he allowed for no flow of them. 'There can be very few worldly circles indeed where they would not be perfectly at ease with their notions,' he wrote, 'whereas I can hardly open my mouth on any particular issue without raising eyebrows & tripping sensibilities.' Maybe I had given him the focus which he hitherto lacked. I will give him this: he was, with respect to me, articulate in his rage.

One evening, in May 1975, after he shouted at my girlfriend over the phone, reducing her to tears, over what I honestly can't remember, I took the typescript of poems he'd given me a month or two before, went to the hotel where he'd just begun his nightshift and threw the pages in his face. They scattered like a gaggle of frightened geese. If he ever spoke again to her in that manner, I said, I'd kill him. I had quite unwittingly, he told me years later, won his affection at that moment. I was, after all, *hombre*.

Sally Purcell's Further Shore

John Clegg

At first glance it would be hard to imagine a poetry less responsive to biographical readings than Sally Purcell's. 'Her spiritual habitat was really somewhere between the thirteenth and sixteenth centuries', writes Marina Warner, and her imaginative landscape holds fast to the same territory. A glance through her titles is enough to get the flavour: 'Loquitur Arthurus', 'Verses for Tapestry', 'One of the Lost Grail-Knights Speaks', 'Guenever and the Looking-Glass'. Her corpus of two hundred and sixty-four poems contains, I believe, only a single mention of an unambiguously twentieth-century object (a typewriter, in 'Oxford, Early Michaelmas Term'). Peter Jay, writing her obituary in the *Independent*, summarises fairly: 'Her poems... give few biographical clues. They are concentrated dramatic lyrics, their matter drawn from classical, Arthurian and medieval myth.'

And yet, every so often, another kind of concern makes itself visible. The poem beginning, 'In a drizzle of tingling light', shorn of its title, would not stand out as presenting a personal or contemporary situation; even with its title ('Ted's') restored, we require Peter Jay's note, that Ted's was private slang for the Duke of Cambridge pub on Little Clarendon Street, before we are any the wiser, and even then the poem's occasion is opaque; I don't think it can be reconstructed. My point is that the poem's classical and Christian motifs do not exist solely for their own sake, as they would have done for the poets Purcell loved best. Myth is, by necessity, public, but these are poems with a private life as well.

There is one myth-complex, in particular, where I think drawing out the personal/mythological connections strongly enhances our reading of the poetry. Merlin – unsurprisingly for a poet so steeped in Arthurian legend – is one of Purcell's recurring figures. In almost all the Merlin poems, I suggest, there is some identification between the magician and Alasdair Clayre, the poet, folk-singer and academic, dedicatee of Purcell's first and second collections. On 10 January 1984, Clayre killed himself, stepping in front of a tube train at Chalk Farm station.

This identification was, I believe, present at least from 'Merlin', in the 1977 collection *Dark of Day*. The poem presents Merlin as the singer able to reconstruct a 'prelapsarian garden', 'away from the ruined / paradise of language': 'we glimpse its dream or ghost again / whenever man like Merlin sings'. Around the period of this poem's composition, Clayre was writing the songs which would appear on his second album, the relevantly-titled *Adam and the Beasts* (released on Acorn in 1978). It is also worth comparing this poem with the slightly later 'To A.C.C.', which shares its odd thirteen-line form – Merlin's song captures how 'branching sun confers / a stately clarity', the poem to Clayre begins, 'Your sunlight strikes through clear windows'.

The identification is confirmed in the poem 'January 10, 1984'. Here are the last three lines of the six-line elegy:

> Branches clash in a dry wind; the twisting path has left him
> far from landmarks where we could meet,
> wandering in the wood of Celyddon.

The (Welsh) myth being invoked here is that of Myrddin Wyllt, the bard of Gwenddoleu ap Ceidio, who went mad after the death of his king at the battle of Arfderydd and fled into the Celyddon (Caledonian) Wood. Myrddin is, of course, the original of Merlin; the title of Purcell's poem is the date of Clayre's suicide; I do not think the identification can be in any doubt here. In the short and obscure 'Merlin (v), for A.C.C.', the only real evidence is the dedication.

If it was simply a matter of 'for *Merlin* read *Clayre*', this would all be of solely biographical interest. But in one other Merlin piece, I think restoring this context substantially improves the poem. This is 'Ripae ulterioris', from *Lake & Labyrinth*; it must have been written shortly after Clayre's death (the collection was published in 1985). Here is 'Ripae ulterioris' in full:

> Edward Thomas learned 'how wind would sound
> After these things should be.'
>
> Merlin foreknew the song he would sing
> When the wall of air closed round him.
>
> The heart rises to recognise
> That secret lightning, leap into a dark
>
> Whose further bank is revealed to love,
> Suddenly, beyond guessing, given.

Both Thomas and Merlin (from the French *Estoire de Merlin*, the source of his imprisonment behind the 'wall of air') were in one sense suicides; it is the literalisation of the metaphor which gives the poem its dramatic charge. 'Leap into a dark' would have been brave enough; the further metamorphosis, by which the Northern line becomes the Styx, is an astounding flash of metaphoric insight, magnetising the poem's other details (the lightning, the wall of air, the sound of wind can all be reconciled to the Underground). Virgil's *ripae ulterioris*, the far bank invisible to the throng waiting to be rowed across the Styx, transforms into the one-bank river of a crowded tube station. And this is achieved without being insisted on, without even being foregrounded, so the reader unaware of the private Merlin/Clayre connection and Clayre's manner of death will necessarily miss it.

I believe the private myth-complex brought to fruition here is ramified through several further poems. The one-banked river, which had never before featured in Purcell's work, becomes a repeated motif, as in the beautiful 'The One-Strand River' (unpublished in her lifetime). *Underground* became a key word (if it occurs in her work before 1985, I haven't noticed it). In 'Terra secreta', 'Centuries afar, another Virgil / knows there is another world / underground, where unearthly time / is lit by the light / of a sun and moon unknown.' In 'Autocrat of the subtle underground world...', Hades watches Orpheus descending; the poet wonders 'can the god know what gift he is giving, / that silence for a theme?'

Shining Muffle

From the Journals, 27 June 2001

R. F. LANGLEY

A day trip (to Diss. to sort out the geography and the places to eat so that we know what we are doing when the Rileys meet us there for a concert in the church in a couple of days. Hot day but blown through by a cool wind. Only The Two Brewers opens early enough to be of use on a concert evening, so it would be better, maybe, to picnic by the Mere. Water up to the concrete brink, with ducks, geese and pigeons... these last flounced up, strutting, ready to mate.

We buy a rug for the landing, warm red, from an Oxfam shop, then drive out) to Hoxne where King Edmund's golden spurs reflected in the brook from where he was hiding under the bridge, and a newly married couple revealed him to the Danes, so he was shot as full of arrows as a pincushion.

The church there has big very faded wall paintings... Seven Deadly Sins as fruit on a tree, each fruit a dragon with the sin in its mouth, and a sprightly young man on top of the tree, as Pevsner says... who is Pride, the church guide says... two devils saw down the tree at the bottom, which seems rather disadvantageous to them but completes the idea of Pride going before a fall. I suppose. An aisle full of noticcboards about the past of the village, links with St Edmund, the Hoxne Hoard. Then the north-east chapel blocked off with benches etc., for restoration.

Against the east wall of it the roof-high tomb, C18, in fact 1742, Thomas Maynard by Charles Stanley... hand on hip, elbow on urn, Roman dress, turning to look out of the window alongside him, which has three lights filled with half-opaque glass but rimmed by a thin line of red glass which is transparent, so he sees close foliage, rising and dropping, all blurred greenish-white, except for thin red precision and clarity round the border. He stares stoically, mind on something else. Strongly cut and posed, all with a dash and grip about it but not a profundity. He seems to have been inserted into the silence not born out of it. The trees he stares into are not his place. He would be doing something else if he could. Odd that the real Roman stuff, the piled coins, the swollen dugs of the leopard, have no thought of his swagger.

We walk back to the little village green where we parked. Two small boys are playing with plastic figures in a cardboard box. Beyond is the bridge over the shallow stream with tall blue-flowering comfrey... that desiccated pale blue that is fading into white but seems to calm the heat of the day with a sense of being old yet rampant.

In the evening as B completes her moderation of A Level English coursework I walk up Silver Stile meadow again, round to the Castle Yard and back. Dusk thickens. Light sinks... deep blue-grey at the bottom, narrowly, then orange and deeper red, fading up to yellow, yellow-green, whiter than that and up to the roof of the sky, an unintense sky-blue still, but with the gusto taken out of it and pale cloud remnants delicately modelled as decorative leftover experiences, finely detailed. The mowed grass glows up and discharges its scent. A hun-dred rooks, over the Hall, puff out in a cloud and swirl and settle away against the red. In the pool, water swishes yet there are only weak ripples, hard to trace back to their source... which could be moorhen under the bushes in the bank.

I find myself walking amidst ghost moths, five or so, knee-height, dwindling, and, looking closer, some of them are yellowish... clearly females who have responded to the flicker of the enamel-bright males. Suddenly a pair clinch on a grass stem and I crouch to see... they are head up, the male against her stomach, as she holds on, arms up above her head, to the grass, his head down under her chin, her wings just overlapping his; then he looses her and drops over and down so he hangs below her, linked at wing tip, and, I take it, abdomen tip beneath. Another pair, a foot away, couple as this pair did originally, and they stay like that, though I expect the male to loose and spin over. I peer at them as darkness intensifies until B appears down the path over the grass and I go with her back round the circuit I had just gone round the other way.

[...]

The valley is windless now, warm and soft, the moths not in evidence, having settled things satisfactorily. People at the village hall have gone quiet, left for home. Cooler tomorrow maybe. The moon is a half-moon now, since I began this volume of journals. It burns and encloses itself in a faint globe of shining.

We had our poetry evening in Norma's garden this week... finishing my 'Still Life with Wineglass' well – using the notions of affects making our life and requiring representation, which binds and is both all that can be adequate and simultaneously what must fall short... as a programme for the poem being written at all, and also as a gloss on what goes on as one pecks at the bundle and the parachutes escape on the alien drift.

(They gave me Adam Phillips' book *Houdini's Box*, wrapped up, with a card Norma brought back from India, as a thankyou for lessons so far, and a hope they would continue. I notice that Harry Houdini had a great trick where he produced an elephant called Jenny out of the air. That helps. The bats were shooting from the boarded end wall of the house, swerving under the tree where we sat at the table, the five of us, with our bottle of wine and bowl of crisps ... we rounded it all off after a couple of hours with a walk round the meadow. Shining muffle.)

edited by Barbara Langley

(transcribed January 2019)

The Window-Ledge

JEFFREY WAINWRIGHT

Let me not look outside today, but ignoring the lightwell,
the lawn, the tree and all the world outside and what
it might mean, look just at my window-ledge
and its horse-brass screwed into a wooden base;
the tea-bell chased with indistinct Egyptian scenes,
its tinkly clapper long gone probably; a dromedary
kneeling, patient, loaded and ready to rise,
a 'ship of the desert'; and three monkeys
insisting they will see, hear and speak no evil,
all these things the last of the brasses we had at home,
'done' in those days, that is polished, weekly.
Then there is a photo of me perhaps aged 4, smiling nicely
in a white vyella blouse, its plastic frame
no bigger than some foreign postage-stamp
and next to that a tin compass, simple enough
but still able to tell me I am facing south.
More colourful, a china model of Jemima Puddleduck
in her blue bonnet with the avuncular Mr Fox
in his brown waistcoat that Audrey gave me
before she lost her mind – fine work from Beswick's
Beatrix Potter collection of the kind she did herself,
and then two late photographs of my Mum
who in latter days found Audrey a good and cheerful friend.
In one she is raising a glass, not really her
but she *is* at Tom's wedding, in the other she is in her chair
with those two long red candles that were never lit
on the shelf behind.   There is another photo of her
with my Dad sitting, I think, near the seaside,
tarpaulined boats in the background,
his arm round her shoulder and both of them
looking so happy.   What else? My only
sporting trophy, Longton Schools Cricket Cup 1954
with Florence Primary and my name incised,
and a plaster William Shakespeare seated.
Sundry other photos: the children playing
water-games in Grandad's garden. That in colour,
and Dad in black and white and tie and pullover
looking away from the camera as advised, and
my mother, my wife, my daughter all together.
That old rectangular wind-up clock in green bakelite
always showing half-past eight, morning or night.

Dollhouse on Fire

SHERI BENNING

AT THE JUNCTION, turn south on Highway 15. Before you reach the former town site of Amazon, turn east down any grid road. Continue until you can see Last Mountain Lake spark on the horizon. Lined with caragana trees planted in the 1930s to anchor the dirt, the fields left in stubble are deer-hide blonde; sky, arterial blue. Keep an eye out for whitetail, maybe moose. Don't be surprised – a sharp-tail grouse might burst out nowhere, a flurry of dun feathers.

No one lives here anymore. This sour land, alkaline, should never have been pressed into cultivation. There's an abandoned yard-site every section or so. Always in the back forty acres, an old barn leans into the pelt of thistle, spear grass, crested wheat, brome. In such a barn I was once badly startled when something coarse brushed my face – the frayed end of a rope tied to a corroded metal hook and pulley, likely where the farmer hung his animals to bleed out before butchering. If you decide to have a look in the house, its windowpanes long shot out, step lightly. Make sure the rotting floor beams can support your weight. You don't want to fall into a dank basement cistern. You'll notice that people leave behind the plainest things. A pocked iron kettle with a regally curved spout; a rain-bloated issue of *The Ladies Home Journal*; a pair of calfskin leather baby shoes, laces tied. I leave these objects untouched. But it's up to you. If you get lost on your way back to the city, look west until you spot the Viterra Grain terminal. You can't miss it. Its immensity is evidence that somebody is still making money out here. In any case, drive towards the terminal. Eventually you'll hit highway.

Rural Saskatchewan is currently undergoing a crisis of place: small-scale, diversified farming has overwhelmingly given way to agribusiness and as the average farm size increases, Saskatchewan's rural communities and natural landscapes suffer. Indeed, a drive beyond the confines of Saskatchewan's cities will take you past abandoned farmyards and villages even as the most unsuitable prairie terrain is put into production.

My preoccupation with the state of agriculture in Saskatchewan stems from my family's experience of maintaining a small mixed farm. In 1998 we were forced to make a choice that was no choice at all. To weather sinking commodity prices and rising input costs, we either had to sell or drastically increase the size of our operation, thereby risking massive debt. Go big or get out. We were not alone in facing such bleak options. According to *The Farm Crisis and Corporate Profits*, a report by Canada's National Farmers Union (2005), in the late 1990s, average net farm incomes dipped below those

endured throughout the Great Depression.

Canadian political economists Roger Epp argues that if there is to be a genuine alternative to corporate agriculture, it will emerge from a regained sense of locality, a striving to 'inhabit a particular place in a serious way' (Epp 318). According to Epp, a deeply felt lived experience of rural places generates a keener understanding of the socio-ecological consequences of economic globalisation on farming. Such an understanding would invariably contradict the propaganda of agribusiness initiatives.

Thus, if the notion that our connection to earth should be dictated by economics, our definition of land value limited to its monetary worth causes harm, amending the damaging effects wrought by agribusiness requires no less than a re-conception of how we relate to place.

*

Contemporary philosopher Edward Casey writes that 'to be at all – to exist in any way – is to be somewhere, and to be somewhere is to be in some kind of place' (*Fate of Place* xi). Place, he adds, is as requisite to being as 'the air we breathe, the ground on which we stand, the bodies we have' (xi). Indeed, for Aristotle, place is prior to all things: 'Everything is somewhere and in place.'

The shunning of place as a crucial concept is manifested in the incessant motion of postmodern life in late-capitalist societies. Too easily discounted is how place exerts its influence on us. Composed of day-in, day-out, fleeting and un-dramatic experiences, cultural geographer Yi-Fu Tuan writes that 'the feel' of place, its singular blend of sights sounds and smells is registered in our muscles and bones (Tuan 184). For Casey, the conjoining of our bodies with environments 'generates the interspace in which we become oriented' (28). Marked and measured by our actions, perceived and remembered, what begins as undifferentiated space transforms into place. Or, as Tuan puts it, when space *feels* familiar to us it becomes places.

Achieved via daily engagement, our times are against this full-bodied sensing of place.

To reassert place's primacy, Casey suggests we don't need to look further than our everyday exchanges. 'Where are you from?' is often the first question we ask upon meeting. Our answers identify us: Saskatchewan, the Rural Municipality of Wolverine Creek, NW 18 36 22 W2nd. Our lives enveloped in the names.

After we sold our farm, NW 18 36 22 W2nd became a symbol for my family that marked distance. In the years

that followed, we were constantly on the move – between regions, cities, jobs, houses. We felt like we had 'no place to go', never lingering anywhere long enough to render a place meaningful. The Greek word for strange, *atopos*, literally means 'no place'. During this time, my parents mostly lived in Saskatoon yet the city remained devoid of significance for them. Alien in their new environment and estranged from the only home they'd ever known, in the evenings my parents aimlessly drove the rural roads surrounding Saskatoon. After driving for a while they'd pull over to walk in some farmer's pasture. Just for the smell of dirt and sage, the sound of spring run-off in the ditches.

Prior to selling the farm, every day before breakfast and then again in the late afternoon, they did chores – fed and watered the animals, gathered the eggs, the milk – the feel of dusk air, the smell of cut clover – a memory formed in the day-to-day, without thought. Casey writes that in residing in a particular place our bodies from 'habit memories,' memories formed by slow sedimentation and realised by the re-enactment of our bodily motions. I think of my parents in Saskatoon, *atopos*, placeless, intuitively following their bodies' drift beyond the city's limits to where they could rest in the familiar: fallow fields, evening light in spear grass.

Feeling like we have 'no place to go' is a desperate circumstance. This is, in part, because we identify ourselves by and with our places. When we lose them, our very selfhood is at stake. A typical response when we experience persistent change is to long for an idealised, unchanging past. As Svetlana Boym writes in *The Future of Nostalgia*, one way we cope with homesickness is to try

and restore the original home: this is a nostalgia which yields to *nostos*, the desire for prelapsarian unity, a return to home (49). Elsewhere Boym writes that, '[t]o feel at home is to know that things are in their places and so are you... the object of longing, then, is not really a place called home, but rather this sense of intimacy with the world' (251).

In 2008, tired of feeling they belonged nowhere, my parents quit their jobs and bought several quarters of land. Thirty years after they started farming for the first time, they started again.

In 2007, my sister, visual artist Heather Benning, restored the interior of an abandoned farmhouse to the date of its abandonment in the mid-1960s. She re-shingled, re-plastered and painted, refurbished the original flooring, and staged the house with vintage furniture and knick-

knacks: a water glass with bright orange flowers left on a kitchen table; a copy of *The Western Producer*, folded open to the grain markets slumped beneath a lamp; crocheted doilies on the chesterfield's armrests; a flannel shirt hanging from a bedroom door. Heather removed the house's north wall and replaced it with plexiglass so viewers could look into the house the way they would a child's dollhouse. She locked the house to discourage entry.

Typically, homey contentment is not the object of our reflection. Rather, we know our households primarily through use; things are handled, smelled and touched, but are too close to us to be seen clearly or discretely – think of how we shade our eyes in moments of embrace (Tuan 144–146). Looking creates distance. By locking the house and keeping the audience at a remove, Heather forced viewers to take note of the domestic bricolage that composes a sense of home, the humble furnishings and their implied web of communal activities.

The affective power of *The Dollhouse* existed in how it spoke to our nostalgia for connectivity. Boym suggests that our culture suffers from acute nostalgia, a 'global epidemic', resultant from the accelerated rhythms of modern life. 'Progress,' she writes, 'didn't cure nostalgia but exacerbated it.' Similarly, globalisation has inspired longing for stronger local attachments. Counterpoint to our fascination with 'cyberspace and the virtual global village, we yearn for community with a collective memory...' (xiv). *The Dollhouse* appealed to our desire for 'continuity in a fragmented world', imparting in viewers the sensation of intimate dwelling even as the possibility of doing so was sealed off from them.

But what does dwelling entail? Consider the words two

apparently antithetical roots: Old Norse, *dvelja* – to linger, delay, tarry; and Old English *dwalde*, to go astray, wander. Dwelling-as-residing and dwelling-as-wandering: every hearth made warmer by departure, by the journey abroad, by the wildness beyond the confines of our built places. Similarly, Casey suggests that built places, if they are to qualify as human dwellings, must satisfy two conditions: they must allow for repeated return and they must possess a felt familiarity, which, in part, arises from reoccupation itself (116).

The dual nature of both dwelling and dwelling places accounts for why it is so devastating when Heather burns down *The Dollhouse*. If *The Dollhouse* suggested *nostos*, the promise of home, appealing to our fantasy for return, then the act of burning it down forces us to linger in *algia*, the pain of longing itself. Reoccupation is made impos-

sible; our homecoming forever delayed.

In the winter of 2014, Heather and filmmaker Chad Galloway documented the burning of *The Dollhouse*.[2] This controlled burn was part of the plan for the project from the beginning. Pragmatically, Heather knew that eventually the house would be broken into; because she could not guarantee the building's safety, she decided that once it was tampered with she would destroy it. But more importantly, with *The Dollhouse* Heather wasn't interested in constructing a mausoleum, a reactive emblem of a past time.

This impulse to rebuild the lost home is characteristic of restorative nostalgia, one of the two kinds of nostalgic tendencies that Boym identifies in our attempts to make sense of our relationships to the past, to our lost homes, to our apparently inexpressible homesickness (41). Boym writes that '[r]estoration (from re-staure – re-establishment) signifies a return to the original stasis, to the prelapsarian moment' (49). The past for the restorative nostalgic is not 'duration but perfect snapshot' (49). At worst, restorative nostalgia is behind resurgent nationalist movements which elide the complexities of historical time by 'engaging anti-modern myth-making and nationalist symbols' (42). In its less extreme forms, restorative nostalgia still has no use for the complications of history – 'the ruins, the cracks, the imperfections' (45). It is manifested in total reconstructions of monuments of the past. Signs of decay are 'freshly painted' in the attempt to achieve the 'original image', to remain 'eternally young' (49).

Fragments overlap in the short film Heather and Chad made about burning *The Dollhouse*; they tug at the viewer's vision. A winter field: power poles, snow and sky. A

scrub of poplars. The house, its rotting shingles. Lace curtains, a vase in a window, a plastic rose. Flames. Skates in the back entrance. A child's laugh up the stairwell. A low drone. Cracks in the plaster. Ash on the bed. Flames climb the wall. Lace curtains, *The Western Producer*, a child's book, a woman's portrait – curl with flames. The rose twists, melts. The drone builds.

Reflective nostalgia, the other kind of nostalgia distinguished by Boym, does not focus on recovery, but rather 'meditates on the passage of time'. As she points out, the word re-flection suggests 'new flexibility, not the reestablishment of stasis' (49). Instead of seeking edenic unity then, reflective nostalgia lingers on the fragments of memory (49). For Susan Stewart, this sort of nostalgic narrative remains inconclusive; it is 'enamored of distance, not of the referent itself' (145).

In the film, as the flames take over, fragments turning to ash, the low drone in the background, which at first recalls a dirge, crescendos into the clash of disaggregated sounds. Performed by Godspeed You! Black Emperor, a Montreal post-rock group, the anarchic soundscape is the sonic equivalent of this place's undoing, its violent dismantling. If previously *The Dollhouse*'s un-restored exterior, the rotten shingles, the weathered siding, suggested to viewers passing time, that the mythical place called home cannot be returned to, the fire makes this distance irrevocable. The home is in ruins. And then, the home no longer exists. According to Boym, this sense of distance, compels the reflective nostalgic to tell her story – to try and make sense of the relationship between past, present and future (51).

The first thing we noticed when we moved to our new farm was how dark it is at night. That fall, while staying with my parents, I got lost driving home after an evening in the city. Did I miss the turn-off for the grid that goes past our farm? Had I gone too far? Not far enough? Panicking, I turned onto a back road, conjuring landmarks to verify my wrong hunch. The road devolved into a dirt path. I'll turn around after the low spot, I thought, but the low spot was filled with water. When Dad found me, I was too embarrassed to try and explain. He was kind. 'The countryside is really dark nowadays,' he said, pulling my car out of the slough with his diesel truck. 'Easy to get lost. No one lives out here anymore.'

It is not too much to say that a seismic demographic shift had occurred in this historic grain-growing region of Western Canada. Indeed, it emptied of people: a drop of 20,000 in a 2008 Statistics Canada labour-force report

(Epp, *We Are All Treaty People* 144). Change in government attitudes towards agriculture – manifested by slashed subsidy programs, trade liberalisation, and the surrender of agricultural research to the private sector – effectively made people obsolete from the land. Rapid advance in agricultural technology further hastened this shift. How else to pay for that eighty-foot air seeder but to increase one's land base? As Wendell Berry observes, 'bigger machines required more land and more land required yet bigger machines which required yet more land and so on' (63). Farmers who survived this period of exodus did so by way of ever-larger machinery and debt-load, not to mention the ruin of their neighbours. The farm had become a factory, wholly adopting the standards of industry to measure performance: speed, efficiency, profitability (63).

So why return? Why participate in this highly exploitive form of farming that is more akin to mining? Why become a low margin contract worker – beholden to seed and chemical conglomerates – in a place that is devolving into a resource plantation (Epp, *We Are All Treaty People*, 161)?

We returned because we remember what it is to love a piece of land – its contours and relief – as more than a place of resource extraction. We remember a kind of labour that joins our bodies to the earth, and the earth sustained us.

We stay because we remember what it is to be part of a community of deeply felt, complex bonds. Because living according to the exigencies of the natural world can breed empathy, unmatched neighborliness. A few years ago, my mom was unwell. When Dad came home to the farm after weeks at her hospital bedside, he discovered that our neighbours had arranged to help harvest our crops. They understood that regardless of anything, the combining had to be done before snow fell.

We returned because between managing inputs and monitoring futures markets, there are fleeting moments of kinship. Several springs ago my dad found a starving kit of foxes in the poplars that surround our farm. Every morning, in the grey light before dawn, he brought them scraps of food. By the end of summer the boldest fox would trot up to Dad and eat from his hand. The foxes still live in our poplars. They keep our yard free of pests. In the evenings we can hear them, shrieking like playing children.

And so we stay, homesick for where we are, making do by dwelling in the fragments, the uncanny doubles of a past time, the ghosts of who we were in a place that no longer exists.

In *Empire Wilderness*, geopolitical travel writer Robert Kaplan foresees the future landscapes of western North America as consisting of 'suburban blotches separated by empty space' (28). This vision aligns with our contemporary assumptions of what constitutes progress: the rural destined for erasure as surely as the future elides the past, economic life, organised along industrial lines, continually concentrated in the hands of the corporate few (Epp, *We Are All Treaty People*, 6).

Almost always, criticism of the direction of mainstream agriculture is pejoratively dismissed as 'nostalgic', the word invoked to signify regression, a too-easy sentimentality for bygone days. Perhaps resistance to corporatised agriculture *is* born of nostalgia, but only if we consider the fuller possibilities of the term. Boym suggests that 'nostalgia is not only about the past; it can be retrospective

but also prospective' (xiv). She arrives at this understanding by way of Henri Bergson who does not view time as simple succession. Deleuze, in his study of Bergson, writes, 'of the present, we must say at every instant that it 'was', and of the past that it 'is', that it is eternally for all time' (*Bergsonism* 55). Rather than conceiving of the past as formerly present moments, Bergson argues that the present and the past are contemporaneous: the past serves as the coexistent condition of the present. As Faulkner puts it, 'The past is never dead. It's not even past'.

Regarding our current cultural clime Tim Lilburn notes that, 'Everything drifts towards money's telos of place-lessness... so how can we be where we are?' (177). Perhaps the affective power of *The Dollhouse* also exists in its capacity to answer Lilburn's question. By laying bare the quiet intimacies and slower rhythms of a past home, *The Dollhouse* suggests to us alternative ways of being in the world. As Boym argues, 'Fantasies of the past determined by the needs of the present have a direct impact on the realities of the future' (xiv). The past can act in the present, open up multitudes of virtual potentialities, non-teleological possibilities for the future. *The Dollhouse* then, more than a reactive monument to the mythical lost home, an irretrievable past, issues its viewers a radical challenge. By its uncanny rendering of intimate dwelling, it asks us to renew our bonds with our environments for the sake of a possible future – nature and culture rejoined in a relationship of harmony.

That nature and culture are not antipodal terms, but rather mutually enlivening is located in the etymology of the word agriculture: *ager*, Latin for field; and *cultura*, cultivation, which, by Late Middle English, provides a root for culture when cultivation of soil becomes metaphor for cultivation of mind. However, within today's mode of agriculture neither term thrives. Land health is exhausted and rural populations are in decline. Wendell Berry argues that this is because our current methods of farming adhere to a far too simple measure, the imperative to produce (5). We have wholly bought into agribusiness standards of bottom line economics, and as a result the field is solely a place for capital gain, an arena for short-term profit (5).

Berry proposes atonement between ourselves and our world, between economy and ecology, by calling for a kind of farming that might acknowledge our interdependence with place. In Berry's alternative vision, farmers would have the means to participate in a kind of agriculture that 'consults the genius of place'. This sort of farming would restore place as foundational; farmers would 'ask what nature would permit them to do... with the least harm to the place and to their natural and human neighbours' (8). Berry adds that the use of the place would invariably change according to nature's response even as the response of the place would change the user. Thus the farmer and his/her land would engage in a relationship of mutual fecundity, a 'conversation' that would bind place and its inhabitants together (8).

Perhaps this promise of reciprocity is another reason why it is devastating to watch *The Dollhouse* burn. In the film, as the house succumbs to flames, an oil well in a neighbouring field comes into view. While the house burns and the oil dirk whines and bobs, we mourn not merely the unrealised dreams of the past, the impossibility of return, but also the visions of possible futures

Tricing

BEAU HOPKINS

An experimental translation of *Trilce* by César Vallejo

I

who
is making all that racket, and won't leave
us sky-enduring islands
    be, excreting our testaments?

    a bit of
courtesy, for christssake. soon
it's late again, day again, lightsout, reveille
    the guano soon
posting a capital gain
o thou treasury
    of preciousest shit

which the sea-stockinged pelican
    drips on the atoll of the heart,
o raft rocking on glass
    -blown waves.

    a bit of
courtesy, oozing white crut
6 p.m. nothing but
    THESE KNOCKOUT B-FLATS.

the peninsula stretches
    out a treelined spine, yawns and
    slumbers on
heedless, of the skullclock's chime.

II

time, a penned

noon wizens, heat-struck.
in the prison yard, a pump
    counts aloud, slonking

    all that's past

the carol of hens scouring it.
daymouth O-ing dry
    tense lips conjugating

tenses with tomorrow

in the warm repose of mere
being. know this now save me
    for then, for tomorrow

slips its name so

what's it called, this thing always
striking us? just the Sameold
    suffering
    name, again.

III

how long till the grownups are home? old blind
Jim is knelling
six. dark already.

    I won't be long, Mother said.

    Aguedita, Nativa, Miguel,
mind yourselves. can't you hear
crossing the courtyard, shrilling their memories
    old crooken souls
bustle in the dark barn, who gave
the poor hens feathering down for the night
    such a dreadful fright.
let's just stay put.
Mother said, she won't be long.

    don't cry. look –
our paper boats (mine's the prettiest!)
the ones we played with until
    the sun fell
and no one argued, and we were good:
they're still tacking on the well
    ready for tomorrow
with their freight of sweets.

    let's do as we were told,
wait, what else. they'll be back soon
with their sorries, the grownups always
    sorry, while they go on ahead
as if little ones left at home
as if we, too,
                    couldn't run off.

    Aguedita? Nativa? Miguel...?
I'm calling, feeling the way, in my dark.
have they gone? no –
    have they?
am I the only one left, in our cell?

A Posy of Pascoli

Giovanni Pascoli

Translated from the Italian by Geoffrey Brock

Fog

Hide what is far from my eyes,
pale fog, impalpable gray
vapor climbing the light
    of the coming day,
after the storm-streaked night,
    the rockfall skies...

Hide what has gone, and what goes,
hide what lies beyond me...
Let me see only that hedge
    at my boundary,
and this wall, by whose crumbling edge
    valerian grows.

Hide from my eyes what is dead:
the world is drunk on tears...
Show my two peach trees in bloom,
    my two pears,
that spread their sugared balm
    on my black bread.

Hide from my eyes lost things
whose need for my love is a goad...
Let me see only the white
    of the stone road –
I too will ride it some night
    as a tired bell rings.

Hide the far things – hide
them beyond the sweep of my heart...
Show only that cypress tree,
    standing apart,
and here, lying sleepily,
    this dog at my side.

Epigrams for Giacinto

Three Grapes

Three grapes, Giacinto, grow upon these vines:
The first is pleasure, and is clear as air;
the next is sweet amnesia. Drink their wines,
    yes – but stop there,

because the third is sleep, in whose dark corner,
keeping a keen-eyed vigil (as you know),
sits grief. And loud is the mute cry the mourner
    cried long ago.

Wisdom

Full of your thoughts, climb to the lonely summits
from which cascades descend and eagles rise,
and there, yourself the center of grey distance,
    stand, and be wise.

Ah, study those unfathomed depths around you:
the farther out the eye of your thought strays,
the nearer comes the thing you're staring into:
    mystery, haze.

Heart and Sky

In the heart, where every vision multiplies
and sky and earth are overwhelmed by space,
a longing may die down, and a hope rise
    up in its place –

the way, in the sky's ocean of deep blue
(where our thought drowns, ascending out of reach)
Alphas may set and, from dark depths, some new
    Omega breach.

Death and Sun

Gaze upon death: that gloomy constellation
that shines against the blackness of the sky,
that sudden word, pellucid apparition –
    translate it, Eye.

You can't. And likewise when you gaze upon
the star that in our lonely sky is burning,
you see – what, Eye? A nothingness of sun,
    a void, churning.

Returning to places where I once shed tears,
I see in those tears now a kind of smile.
Returning to places where I used to smile –
oh! those smiles: how full they were of tears!

My Evening

The day was full of lightning,
but now the stars will come,
the quiet stars. The frogs
croak briefly in the fields.
A gentle joy blows through
the trembling leaves of poplars.
By day, what flares, what claps!
What peace at evening.

Surely the stars will bloom
in that tender, living sky.
There by the cheerful frogs
a stream is softly sobbing.
Of all the dark upheaval
of all that bitter storm,
no sound but that remains
in the damp evening.

And so the endless storm
ends in the song of a stream.
The fragile bolts have left
cirrus of crimson and gold.
O weary sorrows, rest!
The daytime's darkest cloud
has turned to brightest rose
in the late evening.

Such flights of swallows swirling!
Such cries on the calm air!
The hunger of the poor day
prolongs their garrulous supper.
The nestlings' daily portion,
though small, is incomplete –
like mine. What flights, what cries,
in my bright evening!

The bells are ringing: *sleep!*
they say. They sing, they murmur,
they whisper to me: *sleep!*
These voices of blue shadows...
they take me, like lullabies,
back to what once I was...
I'd hear my mother, then nothing,
in the dark evening.

Martial: Some Saturnalia Chestnuts

ART BECK

II, 18

I wheedle, shamelessly, for a spot on your guest list, Maximus.
   You're kissing up to someone else. So, in this, we're equals.
I arrive to pay my morning respects. But you're out, calling
   on patrons yourself. So, we're equals in that respect.
I walk ahead on your rounds, clearing the way like a lackey
   for some pompous princeling. You do the same for someone else.
Once again, we're a pair. It's bad enough being a slave, I'm
   not going to serve one. A king, Maximus, doesn't have a king.

II, 53

You want to escape it all? You say so Maximus,
   but don't. If you really did, here's how it's done.
Be your own master; stop chasing dinner invitations;
   let humble tavern wine quell your thirst. Resist
the glitter of ridiculous Cinna's gold plated tableware.
   Try on my toga for size: Let yourself be captivated
by the plebeian heaven of an ordinary two bit whore.
   So what if your doorway makes you stoop: If
you really want it, if you have a mind to, and strength
   enough, you can live as free as Persian royalty.

VII, 91

Here, for Saturnalia, silver-tongued Juvenal, as you can
   see, are nuts from our little orchard. Alas, the Priapus
who guards the place with his big stiff prick, gave all
   the apples away to dulcet little country sluts.

VIII, 51

Asper's picked a flawless beauty, but Asper's blind. Proof again,
   from a man in love: Beauty's so much more than meets the eye.

X, 20

Not that it's scholarly, or even serious – but
Thalia, my merry muse, please carry this,
not uncouth, small book to eloquent Pliny.
You'll have to navigate, then climb the steep
path out of, teeming Suburra. But after that:

an easy stroll. Once there you'll see sprinkled
Orpheus, presiding over his fountain audience
of enchanted beasts and the regal bird that
snatched up Ganymede for thunderous Jove.
And you'll find Pedo's old cottage from Ovid's

time preserved like a shrine, engraved with
its own little eagle. But don't get tipsy and
eager and rap on the counselor's door at a time
that's not for you. He spends every daylight
minute agonizing over those luminous

court orations that posterity will preserve
and rank with Cicero's. Play it safe and wait
until the evening lamps are lit. That's your
special hour; when the wine is poured, when
the rose is queen, when hair's shaken loose.
Then, even grumpy old Catos recite me.

NOTE

Martial has been popular since the Renaissance, but until a handful of generations ago, as much in the original as not. His short epigrams are accessible to even a beginning Latin student (and particularly attractive to sophomores in search of smut). So it wasn't until the early twentieth century when Latin left the basic curriculum that Martial needed to be translated if he was going to be widely read.

   Prior to that time, translations were often in the grand tradition of 'Englishing': adaptations that recast Martial's lines and even imagery into the translator's current verse models. One example is Tom Brown's seventeenth-century classic which transformed Martial's *Non amo te, Sabidi* into 'I do not love thee, Doctor Fell'. Other adapters included poets as disparate as Ben Jonson, Henry Killigrew and Lord Byron. Post-1960s translations often sought to fill the gap left by previously bowdlerized selections. Martial was ideal for those newly liberated times. But the same rush of freedom that opened English to Martial also liberated translators to enter into their own, time travelling mutations of a poet who seemed as simpatico to their brave new era as he was to his own. In his rollicking 1995 selection, *The Mortal City*, William Matthews 'enthusiastically opted for anachronisms...', in one case renaming 'a greedy Roman mogul Donald Trump, whom I imagine Martial would have delighted to know about.'

Matthews took Martial on an enjoyable tour of twentieth-century New York. Garry Wills, in this century, did something differently similar by crafting his loose adaptations in the eighteenth-century English epigram model Martial arguably helped inspire. But all this Englishing operates at the expense of depriving the reader of the *mea Roma* Martial cast as complicit in his work. And of a proper visit to the eternal City of the patron saint of epigram – a trip akin to the experience good historical fiction can provide. This is, I think, a good enough excuse for yet another re-roasting of these old chestnuts.

It's not a question of greater or less accuracy, rather of giving the Latin challenged reader the *illusion* of reading the original. Translating poetry into poetry is an aesthetic endeavor. Unlike classical studies, it's an art of invisible footnotes and requires the impertinent duet of re-creation. But can't the 'literal' prose versions of classicists give us most of what we need? The Loebs and similar renditions provide invaluable resources. Still. I'd offer that while prose can be translated poetically, poetry (and especially the Latin epigram) doesn't translate into prose. And, I'll ask Martial's Domitian to help me explain.

To wit, that frustrated emperor's quip as quoted by Suetonius: *Princeps qui delatores non castigat, irritat*. The correct and usual prose translation is 'the prince who does not punish informers, encourages them.' But what I think made the line noteworthy to Suetonius is an implicit epigrammatic reading : 'The *princeps* who doesn't whip his informers, spurs them on'. This from a ruler routinely depicted on horseback, who was ultimately 'thrown' by his subjects and his statues destroyed.

A Moment's Life

JENA SCHMITT

Drafts, Fragments, and Poems: The Complete Poetry by Joan Murray (NYRB Poets) $16

BORN IN 1917 in London, England, to Canadian parents, Joan Murray moved to Chatham, Ontario, Canada, when she was a child to live with an aunt, uncle and cousins after her parents divorced, her mother an actor and travelling diseuse, often away, her father rarely if ever present in her life. In an essay, 'Passage on Reading', Murray writes, 'The poignancy of lost mothers and lost children and the sadness in the inevitable wandering of lost things grew quite early with me...'. There was a move to Detroit at age fifteen, and three years later to New York City to study acting and dance before focusing on writing at the New School with Auden. In 1942 she died of a heart-valve infection in Saranac Lake, New York, from the rheumatic fever she contracted as a child. She was twenty-four.

Five years after her death, in 1947, Auden published *Poems* by Joan Murray through the Yale Series of Younger Poets, which makes up the first major section of *The Complete Poetry*; the second is a selection of letters and prose; the third unpublished drafts, fragments and poems from her papers, which are held at Smith College in Northampton, Massachusetts. Her archives have yet to be fully processed – for a time a box went missing, having fallen off a truck in transport, later discovered with a dent.

Farnoosh Fathi is a keen editor who helps to reveal Murray's intelligence and skill, moving as close to the original poems in the first section as possible, rather than the versions liberally edited by a friend of Murray's mother, Grant Code, for the original publication of *Poems*. (He added punctuation where there was none, for instance, separated combined words, fashioned titleless poems with titles, stanzaless poems into stanzas, not unlike the way Mabel Loomis Todd and Thomas Wentworth Higginson edited Emily Dickinson's poetry for publication in 1890.) The letters in the middle section feel like a wedge between two sections of poetry, letters holding open doors to what as a writer Murray was doing and thinking. Words and phrases, images and ideas gather in the first section, echo throughout the letters, continue to reverberate in the unpublished poems of the third section, capturing moments in Murray's life, 'lingering for a moment in the vacuum of a moment's shadow or a moment's life', as she wrote to her friend Helen Anderson.

In 'Poem', Elizabeth Bishop writes, 'art "copying from life" and life itself, / life and the memory of it so compressed / they've turned into each other'. Murray's unfixed life, her unrootedness, is often reflected in her writing. There is a turbulent energy, a constant searching, wandering, figuring, turning, returning, and the spaces left behind are often felt rather than filled. Not even Murray can find them: 'I have looked for my childhood among pebbles my home.'

Many of her poems talk of the sea, the ocean, trees, fields, mountains; of men, women, mothers, fathers, children; of hands, feet, veins, bones, faces; of cities, buildings, rooms, houses, windows, corridors, doors, referring to a sometimes capitalised, sometimes lower-case Builder and Architect (reminiscent of Dickinson's poems and letters about a Master). There is also the Anchorite, the Exile, the Unemployed Woman, letters to a mysterious Baroness. 'The mind of an Unemployed or universal Architect', she explains in a letter, 'epitomised the desire to recreate what is desolated, to rebuild'. In order to make sense of the world around her, she tries to restore a semblance of spaces she recognises or recalls, then lets them collapse under the weight of dense sentences that suddenly warp, splinter, fracture, shatter:

> Like cool stone poured to the palms of a corrupt shivering
> Back to tangle and be lost –

In order to keep pace with Murray, one must leap from word to word, wander around with her a little. In a letter to Auden, she writes:

> I was up to a rather off pursuit this last month and a half. I remember trying to tell you about it last season, and you said, Oh, boy scout stuff! And left me slightly non-plussed [sic]. I shall tell you now. I went out in dungarees and a small pack on my back and covered a scattering of New England states at a tangent. To me, this breaking away and arriving at lands' end is a source of wide-eyed surprise.

And later in the same letter:

> It is always a meeting and escaping. You see I never know what to say to people. That is because I have been mentally asleep for such an endless time. Thank heavens that's over.

No wonder Murray was nonplussed. Perhaps she felt like the women in the 1894 painting *The Garden Court* by Edward Burne-Jones, seated on benches, chairs, the floor, and strangely, inexplicably, asleep. Their arms dangling, heads resting on a lap or a vase, a seat or a post, a thicket of roses thick with thorns behind them, it looks like they've been in a restless sort of slumber a long time, perhaps they've moved through the world that way, neither young nor old, unconsciously quiescent. There is nothing tranquil or natural about their poses. *Wake up*, one wants to say. *That's enough.*

It hardly feels as though Murray slept at all. She seems, in fact, to 'smite this sleeping world awake', as William Morris wrote in response to Burne-Jones's paintings. Along with over a hundred poems, she wrote over seven hundred letters to family and friends, only a handful of which are published in *The Complete Poetry*. She pushed past her disadvantages – inability to write ('It's so utterly bewildering to know just how to write decently somehow'; 'no idea stirred toward a life'), dark moods ('I am drab, grey fog!'; 'Empty has head empty as mood and weak'), and recurring infections that left her bedridden

and near death a number of times before she died – and leapt assuredly, boldly, from thought to thought, idea to idea. The leaps aren't so much pole vaulting as a natural slide, almost imperceptibly, one on top of the other. Often the landscape is superimposed upon the body, the body upon the landscape, hands smooth over its rolling curves, waves have fists, the wind a white heart, and words have the ability to turn and walk away.

Turning into and becoming are not unusual in Murray's work. In 'Vermont Journey', she exclaims, 'Men are women!' Men bear children, women bear trees, children become leaves, the leaves mutter, islands are mothers, seagulls sons. There is a gender fluidity, or perhaps a genderlessness in how Murray views the world, or wants to view it, pushing aside titles and roles into a space that moves amorphously between words and expectations. In the poem 'Ego Alter Ego', she writes, 'You without place or sex', and to Anderson: 'I shall be neither male nor female. I shall be neither God nor Gamin'.

There is an abundance of unmet needs and untold desires, places that are barren, others fecund, 'a night when women's breasts / Hung heaped above my sagging mouth', talk of virginity, lovers, voluptuousness, of panting and sucking and wanting.

Even her epithalamium, a song or poem celebrating a marriage, is a move towards the refreshingly modern. While Catullus, John Donne and Edmund Spenser wrote epithalamiums from the male perspective, and Sappho from a female point of view, Murray's 'Marriage Poem for an Age' is a dramaturgical exchange that voices both women and men, more uncertain and questioning than celebratory, almost a lament:

> Our skirts are so high in blowing. A little wild are the notes
> That keep
> In time, that sing out of the past the tune of the deleted swan.

It's easy to get lost in Murray's fragments, in her 'full-gap-sky', her 'rattled heart', her 'vaster unspecific', her 'V'd wide unbreathing'. I look back through *The Complete Poems* to find 'slattern hills' in a letter turning into 'maddening the slattern' in a poem, 'where people are rivered' becoming the 'rivered summer', 'the veriest seeds of inexplicity', 'the veriest patterns'. Moving from poem to letter to letter to poem upturns the writing in new and unexpected ways. Sometimes it becomes an archeological dig, sifting through words and phrases in search of ancient artifacts, pieces of an amphora or canopic jar, shards of luminescent blue faience, a broken cuneiform tablet from a lost Mesopotamian city. These are as beautifully satisfying as the poems and letters they are pulled from, no need to put the pieces back together. Other times the pieces are ultimately better than the whole.

One hears voices and influences from Housman to Yeats to Le Gallienne, and especially her teacher Auden, whom she was just as eager to dispute as please. There is a similar use of repetition in Auden's 'Prologue XII' ('And the car, the car'; 'Give thanks, give thanks'; 'But love, but love') and the way he anthropomorphised the landscape ('You are a valley or a river bend'), spoke of cities and mythology. There are times when Murray – dare I say it – surpasses Auden in her energy and uninhibitedness, which allowed her a certain freedom to say what she wanted without looking back. Unlike Auden, Bishop or Marianne Moore, who continually edited their poetry throughout their lifetimes, Murray wasn't afforded such time or opportunity. She ends one poem (many of her poems are untitled) in an almost modern-day teenage-speak 'As if', her thoughts trailing off, never to be revisited. There is an unedited roughness there, some poems end without punctuation, some do, sometimes she moves in such tangents that it is difficult to understand what she is moving towards.

Her heart-racing, fist-clenching frustration is often palpable ('A child is born not out of your womb, woman, / But out of the worn centuries of man'), her lines tightening until the point of breaking: 'Of all the eyes that drub along the surface will there be one / catch beyond the the moment'. The two the's no mistake.

Sometimes the frustration is the reader's: 'with only the thread of a self felt strand balancing out the fragile spanning'.

In André Kertész's silver gelatin print *Bird in Flight* (1960), what is perhaps a fire-escape-ridden building looks more like a darkly tunnelled underground. Murray tunnels, pummels, pushes her words deeper, repeating and fragmenting and speaking out more often, more intensely, as though she were trying to get to 'the end of the end'. Her repetitions, though frequent, are far from belaboured:

Mother mother my heart is like twin infants
Suckling dew out of grass
When there should be roisterous breasts
When there should be cornstalks whacking
Their vivid sweep into the core that barren bares
Tombs tombs more tombs

Like an incantation or hymn ('Be careful of dead places. / Be careful of dead places'), these repetitions have a haunting, mind-hitching effect, a palilalia-like echo that moves through the page as though through a cave, one that, to my mind, looks like Lascaux, with its Magdalenian wall paintings of aurochs and deer.

One can feel the aftermath of the world wars in poems such as 'This Makes for War!', 'London sits with her hands cupped...', 'The Coming of Strange People', written on the day of Holland's invasion, and 'Poem': 'The speed of planes was still upon the noon... Windows were slammed and men stood in circles of eternity.' Others reflect the prejudices and anti-Semitism of the time, with references to cripples ('always the cripple', a term also used by Auden), 'the simple people of Vermont', 'the fat Jew fellow with the nose', a 'phlegmatic Indian', and '(*In the voice of a young black boy, sung to a lute*) / Black people, you listen to me...', which reveal naïve, stereotypical views unfortunately fueled and accepted by many.

When William Meredith reviewed *Poems* in the September 1947 issue of the US magazine *Poetry* (which was thirty-five cents each or four dollars a year at the time), he wrote:

As brilliant and moving as [the poems] are, they frequently betray the imperfections of unfinished work, quite a different thing from unsuccessful work, but to the reader just as distressing. Insoluble ambiguities of syntax, unjustifiably abrupt transitions, and what the editor calls 'makeshift' words, inserted temporarily to fill out the shape of a poem, occur in several poems, and will keep them from being as widely read as they are entitled to be. These imperfections increase the difficulty of certain poems, already having a fine toughness of fibre, to the point where they become a chore to solve.

Nothing feels makeshift or made up in the words Murray chose to combine. Her inventive neologistic compounds – deadawake, riverrun, selfadvent, desertsea, unbornhour, mistressthoughts, coiledblue – are weighted just enough to keep a door propped open. Such pushed-together words alter sounds, intonations and stresses, hence the tension in a line. It's a subtle but brilliant difference. When 'coiled blue' becomes 'coiledblue', a sudden tightening occurs, what appears to be a spondee turns towards an iamb. More turning into and becoming.

Her use of hyphenated words such as hung-sky and grey-swung are just as effective. Along with strong active verbs (everything from straddling, shivering, tangling, puttering and riddling, to perking, trammeling, rilling, rollicking and gutting), they insist on movement, helping to propel lines and ideas forward. Nothing is left to stagnate or settle or slam shut. There is no lulling sentimentality to rest upon, only a purity of thought, and a toughness that isn't so much obdurate as relentlessly imaginative and complex, as quick and clever and unconventional as ever. 'I find that like both sea and air I am two things,' writes Murray in another untitled poem, 'Crystal and clear and at the other hand sweet mad.'

Paul Klee said that '[a]rt does not reproduce the visible; it makes visible'. Murray may have written about 'inlocked worlds' and 'inlocked hands', of an anchorite living in an irreversible reclusory complete with a walled-up door, but she continually pushed against those boundaries and limitations, against the unknown. It is little wonder, then, that in Murray's world the body becomes the landscape, something more substantially durable and enduring.

'It is a bit worrying that I so rarely feel even a momentary belonging', she confides in Auden. While Yeats talked about poetry as the thinking of the body, there is also a sense of what Emerson called 'alienated majesty' in Murray's writing, suffused as it is with veils and sphinxes, hieroglyphs and symbols, seals and bones, something Delphic, distinguished, mysterious, that needs deciphering: 'An illusion of dream veils the symbol of the symbol, / Puts its seal upon the head, a birthmark to the bone.' The kinds of marks that appear and disappear, disappear and reappear, or are always there, hidden or in hiding.

When the windows break and walls crumble in a childhood home she can no longer see let alone find, or wars turn neighbourhoods into rubble, Murray speaks out again and again:

Believe me, my fears are ancient,
And I deal in ancient patterns
Like the burst into spring I am defiant

In this way, she had no choice but to make a space of her own, one that continues to move propitiously past the temporal. As Thoreau said:

We should live in all the ages of the world in an hour; ay, in all the worlds of the ages. History, Poetry, Mythology! – I know of no reading of another's experience so startling and informing as this would be.

Or as The Shades chorus in 'Orpheus: Three Eclogues', the only poem Murray saw published in her lifetime: 'Orpheus, springing towards the wonder of the dead / undead'.

Three Fables

James Tate

A Shift in the Attic

I was swinging on the porch when all of a sudden I fell over
and hit the floor. I don't know how it happened, but I stood up and
brushed myself off. I stood there for a minute, dazed, and felt myself all over
to see if I was hurt. I seemed to be all right. I tested the swing to see
if it was broken, but it wasn't. Maybe it was an earthquake. I walked into
the kitchen and a teacup fell on my head. I thought that was mighty
strange. I swept it up. I went back into the living room and sat down
on the couch. I picked up the newspaper and read about a little girl who
fell into a hole and was never seen again. It made me sad. How could
that happen? There's an end to everything. My couch was sagging. I'm
going to hit the floor, I thought. And then I did. I got up and looked around.
This wasn't my house at all. Yes, it was. There was the little penguin
on the wall, and the walrus beside him. I recognised everything, down
to the little worm on the floor. I moved to the chair beside the window
where the light would be better. Now I could see my hand, not that I wanted
to. It was all gnarly and grey. The chandelier was shaking. Then suddenly all
was quiet. My hands were glowing and so were my cheeks. I felt healthy and
wise. I looked over at the staircase to the attic and there stood a moose.
I nearly jumped out of my skin. But the moose was calm, just looking
around. He walked over to me. There was a bowl of cookies on the table
and I started feeding them to him. He seemed to really like them. When
they were all gone, I walked into the kitchen. He followed me. I
opened the refrigerator and grabbed a head of lettuce and started to feed
it to him. When that was gone I gave him a bowl of spinach, and so on.
We were becoming great friends. Finally, there was a knock on the door.
A man stood there and said, 'That's my moose.' I said, 'No, it isn't. It's
my moose.' He was really mad. He said, 'It isn't your moose. It's mine.'
'I swear it's mine,' I said. And while we were arguing, the moose walked out
onto the porch, jumped the rail and was gone, never to be seen again.

The Execution

The potboiler came back into the cave and said, 'There are no rabbits anywhere today. I guess we'll have to slaughter one of our pigs, precious though they may be.' 'We can't do that. We'll never find a pig again. They are a dying species,' Ham said. 'But what are we going to eat? If there are no rabbits, we have no choice but to slaughter the pig,' Tree said. 'We could eat Bob. He's no use to us,' Samovar said. 'That's a great idea. Bob does nothing but eat our rabbits. He never hunts, he brings us nothing to eat. His time is up,' Ham said. 'Let's go get him,' Samovar said. And so they all gathered and went in search of Bob. When they found him asleep under the banyan tree, Potboiler said, 'Wake up, Bob, it's your turn to feed us.' Bob rubbed the sleep from his eyes and said, 'What do you mean? I can't feed you. I have no food.' 'No, you don't understand. We want to eat you,' Samovar said. 'Don't be silly. You can't eat me. I am one of you,' he said. 'You contribute nothing,' Ham said. 'I'm a wit, I'm really quite funny,' Bob said. 'We're talking about victuals, you know, food,' Potboiler said. 'Well, I guess I'm on the slight side there,' he said. 'Therefore we're going to eat you,' Samovar said. 'Oh, I see, it's becoming quite clear now,' Bob said. 'Who's going to do the job is the only question?' Ham said. 'I'll do it. I never liked Bob anyway,' Samovar said. 'Thanks a lot,' Bob said. 'Well, it's true,' he said. 'Let's not break into petty scrabbling,' Tree said. 'That's true, this should be a dignified execution,' Potboiler said. 'Let's get on with it,' Ham said. 'Bring me the sword,' said Samovar. 'We only have a knife and fork,' Potboiler said. 'What kind of execution is that?' Samovar said. 'It's a dainty one,' Ham said. 'I don't like a dainty execution,' said Samovar. 'I think I do,' said Bob. Potboiler said, 'I have an idea, let's just each of us have a popsicle and call it quits.' 'Yeah, that's a good idea. Let's just have popsicles,' Ham said. 'Sounds great to me,' said Bob.

The Shepherd

Betsy fell out of an airplane one day and floated down into the trees. She was all right except for a stick stuck between her toes. She stayed in the trees for several days until she was rescued by a sheep farmer one morning. He took her home and removed the stick between her toes and gave her a hot toddy. She fell in love with him and they were soon married. She made him soup every day which he thanked her for as though it was the first time he had tasted it. He asked about her family and she said she had none. She asked about his and he said he had many, though he said he never saw them. She asked him why, and he said, 'Sheep.' Harold smoked his pipe most of the day. When she asked him why he smoked it, he said, 'Sheep.' It was the same answer he gave to everything. But he loved Betsy. You could tell that by the way he wrapped the blanket around her in the evening. He never wanted her to be cold, especially at night. He would build a fire and make her sit by it every night. Then he would sing to her, the gentlest lullabies. She would fall asleep like this every night. In the morning it was different. He was all business, feed the sheep and water them, clean out their cages. It was a long day's work. A break for lunch and little else. But when he came home from work he always asked how she was, how her day had gone. And she always told him it was fine. She asked him if he ever took vacation. He said he had never thought about it. Who would take care of the sheep? She said he could hire someone. Surely there was someone with that talent. He said he would look into it. A week later he said he had found someone. And so they took a trip to North Dakota a month later. They had rented a cabin on a lake. Betsy loved it. They fished all day and cooked what they caught on an open fire at night. Harold had never been so happy. When it was over they returned home, but the sheep were gone. They couldn't believe it. They searched everywhere, but they were gone. The man they had hired was a thief. What would they do now with no animals to tend to? They decided they would be happy without them. They would be poor, but happy. And if they ever caught up with the thief they would thank him. And then Harold would kill him.

Four Poems

JOHN CLEGG

The Nordeney Dykemaster

Little inlet, my legitimate
        backwater, low tide
will about bear my front wheel's weight but not quite
        so I make the jolly
Wattwurm jump out of its sandcast
as I visit, four miles off, friend lighthousekeeper.

Lighthousekeeper
        is manoeuvring
a giant bulb upstairs, but has a candle
burning on his kitchen table
        I keep company.
Friend candle, Herr Wineglass, lost moth,

let's call each other *du*. Mud pools
disintegrate to mist, it is
        an alright night.
I scan a posted crib of signals for 'distress'
in fifty languages, flag language, wind,
        bird language:

        once, a calm day
on the dyke, I watched high overhead a fulmar
being dragged backward by something like a riptide –
        his big
wingtips found no purchase anywhere.
And not a breath of wind at human level!

So my proper lookout is this shallow camber,
coaxing storms into the over-
        or the undercurrents.
Lighthousekeeper, dredge upstairs for souls
        drowning or floundering – I'll
tend below this inlet, wineglass, candle.

The High Lama Explains How Items Are Procured for Shangri-La

'Every third decade or so, a convoy of porters –
such as, my major domo informs me, you yourself
once belonged to – receives an unusual commission:

the expedition they are carrying for is to find itself
indefinitely delayed (you know how easily such an excuse
can be fabricated), and one small item of cargo

is to be lost – a piano, some bannister ends,
a ceremonial urn of the sort you were admiring earlier
in the stairwell, it might be, it might well be –

once this is missing beyond all relocation
the caravan picks up and shambles on: we trust
up here to the natural drift of unmoored objects,

a convoy travelling crossways some years later
ditches a satchel of pillowcases down a crevasse,
a herdsman finds an entire silver service, minus

the fish-knives, stowed under scree on a hillside:
either he leaves them, then creeps back at night
to find them already vanished; or he uses them

all his life and they pass by bequest
up the valley into the blue mountains already mentioned
when we were discussing this place's preciseish location.'

The Ozymandias Protocol

Boundless and Bare, two detectives,
Investigate who stole the trunk.
They conclude that the limbs were defective
But the sculptor by now's done a bunk.

So they pull in an elderly tourist
To establish the dates of his trip.
He is full of complaints, but seems sorest
That a big head's been giving him lip.

So they question the head, Bare and Boundless,
Sunk in sand, which is deeper than thought.
'Your suspicions are all of them groundless',
It growls. 'All your work's come to naught.

You're welcome to both kiss my sandy ass;
Then God help me you'd better be leaving.
Or you'll find out what pull Ozymandias
Still has, in the land of the living.'

They head back to lost pets and divorces,
Expense accounts which they can pad,
Bent DAs, heiresses with horses
Who have gone to the drink or the bad –

And keep themselves out of antique lands
Where wind blows the dust into devils
Where sculptors mock kings with their weak hands
And where only the sand's on the level.

Fen

The whole fen seemed on a tilt, at an angle of about five degrees on an axis orthogonal to the dyke path. It was dusk. Time and light were draining from the back of the landscape toward us. Over Ely, whose cathedral we could just make out on the horizon, it was almost midnight, and getting perceptibly darker. Where we were it was still warm, about six o'clock, the remnants of sunset lingered impossibly. All that moved was a small girl leading between stationary caravans her flock of named geese, whose daytime job was to crop the caravan lawns, heads cocked on one side scissoring grass an inch from ground level, not snatching it up in clumps like ruminants. We knew they were named because we heard her calling them, one by one, home over the cattle grid.

Three Poems

L Y N E T T E   T H O R S T E N S E N

Ephemera

I remain non-committal about admitting that happiness
is ephemeral

the happiness that is deliberately infrequent
the most glancing of moments

the not being caught in the storm
the swollen ankle less swollen today

an astonishing photograph of your son in Ha Long Bay
a complicit smile from a stranger in a bus

in between is
the refugee thing that isn't getting any better
president 45
the tomato plants destroyed by a hail storm
which are not, however, a wholesale forest fire in
Portugal

then, there is the unexpected laughter
of my serious doctor friend
the unveiling of a perfectly furry yellow peach
and you
my French husband who longs to come home

the filigree gates swing wide open to the valley
misunderstood by most, but
who cares? who cares?

the wolves no longer howl here
and tonight we shall walk to the theatre.

ANZAC Day

Villers-Bretonneux, France, 2018

The weather hasn't helped
but maybe that's about right.
Well, we all say, what's a seven hour wait in the mud
compared to what they went through?

The organisation is slick.
Thousands of plastic ponchos are thoughtfully provided
for the rain.

We see the ANZAC dawn ceremonies in Australia
on the big screen until this one begins,
strangely anticlimactic,
the bugler messes up the Last Post.

We shiver en masse and only
Prince Charles is allowed an umbrella.
An Australian major general
goes hoarse reading out the names of the
dead young men.

Endless documentaries pay sophisticated homage
to the horrors of war.
The French Prime Minister gives a better speech
than the Australian one does.

When we leave the crowd and
go to a different military cemetery
where my great uncle is,
I finally weep.

The wind offers no mercy and the cypress trees
in front of the yellow fields
bend sideways.

There are no poppies here, paper or otherwise.
The visitors' book shows no one has been here
in months.

Ernest is buried with New Zealanders
but not with his brother,
who is in another cemetery up the road.

A Tale of Two Nests

An absurd distance from home
and my adored Aurora Australis sky,
quite the other end of the earth in fact, I
ran there in all thoughtlessness,
years ago now
decisive and
never coming back.

Here in this not so new life is a
vast garden with small birds in muted colours that don't
shriek.

The first nest, with three nestlings suffered
the double indignity of sunlight and human curiosity
as the rock was rolled away. One little tiny thing
didn't make it and my husband's concocted
prayer (even though he's an atheist) as he buried it under the
Hazelnut tree, despite ourselves,
touched something in us.

The second nest, better camouflaged
avoided our gaze and even though
the birds sang more sweetly, I couldn't
stop seeing those other little feet in the air,
the eyes squished shut and the miniscule beak
open and awry.

The same afternoon,
France won the World Cup soccer
and the whole country
exploded in Gallic joy, but not in our tamed hamlet.

My son, calling from Ha Long Bay, Vietnam,
chided me for not being on the Champs Elysées
or somewhere, or anywhere at all more exciting.
I did wonder what sort of slow moving
old woman I had become.

Liking A. E. Stallings

'Matrona Docta' and Metrical Poet

N. S. THOMPSON

SHORT BIOGRAPHIES DELIGHT in saying Stallings studied classics in Athens, Georgia and now lives in Athens, Greece, married to the journalist John Psaropoulos with whom she has two children. Born in Decatur, Georgia in 1968, she later did postgraduate work at the University of Oxford. *Like* (Farrar Straus Giroux) is now her fourth book of poetry, the first three having won major awards and grants in the United States. For British readers she writes the occasional 'Freelance' article for the *Times Literary Supplement*, where her poems also appear, and is perhaps remembered for her candidature for the Chair of Poetry at Oxford in 2015, when it was won by Simon Armitage.

As a largely metrical poet, her work occupies a link with tradition, but also opens up a historical space that offers a fascinating horizon for the reader as well as offering a touchstone for the creative act. It could be argued that such a referential link is irrelevant today in that in order to understand the contemporary world we need only today's references, today's things and today's ideas. The notion of 'the poetry of Now' goes back to D. H. Lawrence's essay 'The Poetry of the Present' (published as preface to his *New Poems*, 1920) where he says that 'the seething poetry of the incarnate Now is supreme'. It is still a view to which many adhere, but in dealing purely with the present, there is always a danger of it rapidly becoming the past and with the pressing speed of change the example of history becomes forgotten, primarily because it becomes illegible. We do not know how to read or interpret it. If we forget history at our peril, it is because we lack a perspective on it. The idea of shape allows us that perspective and that, in turn, allows us to see history more clearly.

What is more, the perspective of history brings an inclusiveness that draws people together and is civilising. And one of today's problems is that we have no feeling for a civilised view: we seem to enjoy chaos, as if the ultimate thrill is the transgressive feeling of a biker on a chopped down Harley-Davidson gunning freely and at speed through town and desert with no thought but for that moment. This is indeed a tantalising prospect, a freedom eulogised by the late Thom Gunn in his 1957 poem about Californian bikers in 'On the Move':

> In goggles, donned impersonality,
> In gleaming jackets trophied with the dust
> They strap in doubt – by hiding it, robust –

But in contrast to Gunn's skilful rhyming the 'hardiness' of these riders has 'no shape' and the restless energy they possess in a 'valueless world' merely leads to the conclusion of the last line, 'One is always nearer by not keeping still'. This was also the world of cinematic anti-heroes portrayed by Marlon Brando and James Dean.

A world that could be characterised not as rebels without a cause, but – in contrast to the previous generation of the 1940s – *heroes* without a cause.

But whether we like it or not, heroes and heroines have been our touchstones throughout history. And no matter how heroic, they also remind us of our humanity because their flaws. We may not be able to identify with the heroic part, but we can certainly identify with the flaws. And our heroes and heroines can also be tragic. The tragedy often brought about by that flaw, that *hamatia* first identified by Aristotle in his *Poetics*. But what is this flaw? Is it not having a strong enough sword arm? Is it not having enough patience or fortitude? The judgement lies in what Aristotle defines as 'character' in a play, that is, 'that which reveals the moral purpose' of those characters.

Reading the poetry of A. E. Stallings gives one the feeling of travelling in a well-steered craft over the turbulent waters of life. Indeed, it is from such a position that the turmoil can be fully represented and perceived if not finally understood. And if Stallings's poetic craft is so firm on the choppy waters of life it is because it is well freighted with both the sense of history and moral action. One would like to use the metaphor 'anchored' in or even 'grounded in', but this would give the wrong impression, because there is a fluid movement at work that glides effortlessly from the example of history into a relevance and example today. And this is aided by the perspective she achieves.

Thus from her very first book *Archaic Smile* (1999) we see the largely Ancient Greek past brought to life in a vibrant and touching manner. This is no stilted archaising, the life of these characters is edgy because often seen on the edge of death. A brief sample of titles must suffice: 'Hades Welcomes his Bride', 'Persephone Writes a Letter to her Mother', 'Eurydice Reveals her Strength', 'Medea, Homesick', 'Ariadne and the Rest', 'Daphne', 'Arachne Gives Thanks to Athena', 'Tithonus'. For this last poem, the poet alludes to the tragic figure not as Tennyson does in his dramatic monologue where the Trojan prince appeals to Aurora (goddess of dawn) who had given him immortality but forgot to add immortal youth, but rather we have a familiar domestic setting of an aged relative:

> Do not look at me, and let me turn away
> When you set me by the window in my chair,
> Cover me with blankets, give me breakfast on a tray
> (Soon the sky will glow with your red hair).

The last line in this first quatrain highlights the poignancy of decrepit age with both a reference to the goddess and the actuality of a fine day lighting the carer's red hair.

This touchstone of classical Greek mythology is never far away, but many of the poems reference death and smaller tragedies in an assimilable way. It is as if the poet wants to elicit the sad smile of recognition rather than to shock a reader presumed to be lethargic in an after-dinner sleep.

In many ways, Stallings can be seen like Athena, not only for her human wisdom, but for rising fully formed. From the beginning she exhibits a mastery of form in quatrains, villanelles, monologues and the sonnet. On the other hand, looking at her work as a whole, it is also like seeing an ancient city developing out of its humble wooden structures to becoming a brick and marble splendour.

Two further collections were *Hapax* (2006) and *Olives* (2012) where the same general themes are explored but in new and arresting ways. What emerges is a playfulness away from a Southern Gothic preoccupation with the operatic themes of love, family and death – however well and elegantly handled – to a greater engagement with time and change as we experience it.

The title of this latest collection *Like* is taken from the poem 'Like, the Sestina' which has as epigraph 'With *a nod to Jonah Winter*', the American children's author and illustrator. The poem is not strictly a sestina, in that every line ends with 'like', but rings semantic changes on the word, together with word formations on which it is based (such as 'dislike', 'money-like', 'alike') as well as the many parts of speech it can form, from the normative adjective, adverb, conjunction, noun, preposition and verb to uses prevalent today, such as the colloquial quotative (She was like, 'Hold on, a moment'). The source of the poem is the 'Like' button which has become so crucial a marker in social media sites and Stallings rings the changes on it in a deftly witty style that is a new development in her work.

She has always had a sharp eye, but at the same time has written mainly from a distance, what might be called a middle distance. This recalls the famous passage in the opening to Book II of Lucretius's *De Rerum Natura* quoted by Bacon in his essay 'On Truth' where speaks of the service that distance provides:

> The Poet, that beautified the Sect that was otherwise inferior to the rest, saith yet excellently well: *It is a pleasure, to stand upon the shore, and to see ships tost* upon the Sea: A pleasure to stand in the window of a Castle, and to see a Battaile, and the Adventures thereof, below: But no pleasure is comparable to the standing upon the vantage ground of Truth, (*A hill not to be commanded, and where the Ayre is alwaies cleare and serene,* And to see the Errours, and Wandrings, and Mists, and Tempests, in the vale below: *So alwaies, that this prospect be* [seen] *with Pitty, and not with Swelling or Pride.* (see also *The Advancement of Learning*, Chapter 1)

It is not without coincidence that Stallings also translated Lucretius into fourteeners, a prosodic tour de force, published as *The Nature of Things* (Penguin Classics, 2008). And she found Bacon's words tested when she was a volunteer to help the refugees arriving in Greece and wrote 'Empathy':

> My love, I'm grateful tonight
> Our listing bed isn't a raft
> Precariously adrift

As we dodge the coast guard light...

and while she feels for the plight of these victims of 'smuggling rackets' she concludes with brutal honesty and brutal pun on 'die' (as it were 'to long to be with'):

> Empathy isn't generous,
> It's selfish. It's not being nice
> To say I would pay any price
> Not to be those who'd die to be us.

And we see the poet examining her domestic life in poems addressed to her daughter Atalanta, to 'Summer Birthdays' and even to the minutiae of a stain, a shattered glass, sea urchins, a pull toy, scissors and a pencil that – unlike ink – has the blessing of erasure and elicits the comment:

> All scratch, all sketch, all note,
> All tentative, all tensile
> Line that is not broken,
> But pauses with the pencil,
>
> And all choice multiple,
> The quiz that gives no quarter,
> And Time the other implement
> That sharpens and grows shorter.

The examination of these implements and other objects or living things reminds one very much of the Metaphysical poets who could wring such charming or poignant observations from a pair of compasses (Donne), a flower or pulley (Herbert), a vine or daffodil (Herrick). The secret, if there be one here, is in the use of wit, which an online dictionary defines as 'the keen perception and cleverly apt expression of those connections between ideas that awaken amusement and pleasure'. Samuel Johnson, who coined the term 'metaphysical' was against the farfetched comparison, but clearly many poets have shown that it is effective and here, in Stallings's work, we see it in a serious context with Time and the humble pencil. The interest is in the avoidance of the potentially comic.

What comes to the fore in this latest collection is the word 'play'. As we have seen, there is an adventurous ludic quality in 'Like, the Sestina', and this is mirrored in the way she absorbs the male heroic tradition out of Homer or the Greek playwrights and incorporates it into her work. This is not only respecting a tradition that goes back millennia but is truly creative. Where a feminist might simply decry a male (heroic) perspective as toxic masculinity, Stallings treats it with a subtle playfulness. One of the best examples is in 'Cast Irony' about the washing of a skillet that should not be washed – or else heat dried immediately if it is. But washed with soap:

> Now it is vulnerable and porous
> As a hero stripped of his arms
> Before a scornful chorus.

What is also evident in her work is – as here – the untroubled use of allusion. Often this is married to the theme of similarity, or more strictly, the yoking of dissimilars in the Metaphysical tradition, but we see in several poems that are based on the simile where the poet effort-lessly uses the male heroic world for her own purposes. 'Epic Simile' depicts a Homeric charioteer in battle while a female figure of the hero's death anachronistically 'beads on him like a sniper's sights' but then 'leaps away like luck' at the 'clean report of a cracking poplar branch' and he's left with his sweat and blood but also the snow-capped mountains in the distance. In 'Half an Epic Simile Not Found in Hesiod' the poet self-deprecatingly describes a visit to the hairdresser of 'a faded blonde / On the brink of middle age' where all she wants is:

> a color adjustment,
> For rays of honey to eclipse the grey,
> And for the light to lengthen just a little.

Again we see a poignant pun on 'light'. Thirdly, 'Similes, Suitors' is in two parts: the first opens with a depiction of a modern Aegean shoreline where an illegal catch has been dumped among the plastic bottle caps and likens it to the sight of Penelope's suitors in the *Odyssey* after the eponymous hero and his son have dealt with them. The second half takes their shades into the halls of Hell as a metaphorical colony of disease stricken bats.

What we also see here is a venture into forms that go beyond the lyric. Usually her poems are no more than a page or two. A visit to a literary festival in Cyprus has result-ed in 'Cyprian Variations' a diaristic set of twentyfour short poems ordered according to the Greek alphabet. Indeed, the collection is ordered alphabetically. But central to the collection is the sequence of thirty-six stanzas in *ottava rima* which bring the collection's themes of time, ageing and memory together in 'Lost and Found'. She first engaged with the stanza form in her contribution to *A Modern Don Juan: Divers Cantos for these Times by Divers Hands* (Five Leaves, 2014), where sixteen contemporary poets each wrote

a canto narrating the adventures of Byron's hero brought up to date in the twenty-first century. The exercise proved a happy discovery for many (both poets and readers) that narrative poetry could still be written today. The narrative element is again strong in 'Lost and Found' and follows the structure of a medieval dream poem, starting with the poet searching unsuccessfully for some piece of a toy vital to her son and her stroppy rejoinder to his complaining about the loss. As she dreams that night she meets a shad-owy figure in a landscape who says, 'This is the valley of the moon /Where everything misplaced on earth accrues, / And here all things gather that you lose' and she takes the poet on a Dickensian tour through the past by means of the objects they find in the valley. Metrically, Stallings does not miss a beat and the reader is taken up with the strange oneiric journey that is fortunately not as harrowing as Scrooge's in *A Christmas Carol*.

Although the poetry has a distant base line in Ancient Greece, it is brought up to date in modern Greece with 'Refugee Fugue' a four-part sequence with many sub-headings where metrics are abandoned in favour of the found discourse of other forms in 'Aegean Blues', 'Char-on', 'Aegean Epigrams' and 'Appendix A: Useful Phrases in Arabic. Farsi / Dari, and Greek'. The latter section is literally taken from a *Guide to Volunteering* published in Greece in 2016. The phrases begin with kindly greetings and offers of help, through to personal details and end on the chill tones of a bureaucracy that can stretch no further in its aid.

In sum, Stallings is a poet writing about her life and times not from her personal gender perspective or for her gender alone, but in a historical tradition of appealing to the witness of history, even in regard to domestic minu-tiae, and to its moral judgement on the deeper questions of right and wrong. It exhibits a heroic effort, if a playful one, and shows a mastery of poetic form and judgement.

From the Archive

Issue 146, July – August 2002

CHRIS WALLACE-CRABBE

From a contribution of three poems alongside 'Reflective Insulation' and 'Language of the Eye'. Fellow contributors to this issue include John Ashbery, Caroline Bird, Evelyn Schlag, Edwin Morgan and Alison Brackenbury.

INDOOR YACHTING

Indoor Yachting

Has any mere scribbler
ever spotted or caught

that fine dramatic gesture
by which a homebody

standing down at the bed-end
flourishes a wide clean sheet and

blows it out like a spinnaker
so that the far end

will flutter down in place
where a pillow will be,

once again
getting it right?

Two Poems

STEWART SANDERSON

The Solan

Goose
or gannet, 'whose
    smell is so powerful that he is'
    under no circumstances
        'cooked within doors', is the largest

sea-
bird of any
    to be found in the North Atlantic
    combing the oceanic
        distance in search of sustenance

or
perched by the score
    on perilous ledges high above
    the waves as they surge and shove
        at the foundations of the land.

Scott,
a writer not
    to be deterred by powerful smells
    insofar as his novels
        required, describes the 'relishing'

taste –
fish interlaced
    with pheasant – of a well-smoked solan
    which till recently formed an
        important part of our cuisine.

In
Boece's *Latin*
    Chronicle, or else the translation
    into Scots made by one John
        Bellenden, we read how the Bass

Rock –
that trachyte block
    three hundred million years or so
    in age, covered with guano –
        bears 'an incredible noumer

of'
(hard not to love
    his spelling) 'soland geis; nocht unlik
    to thir fowlis' (with a stick
        I could eat such words) which Pliny

calls
'see ernis': squalls
    of them rising and falling round their
    black fastness; filling the air
        with the dissonance of their song.

To Artio

Because my love is like a bronze bear shambling
through thorn bushes towards a Gallo-Roman
lady, I, Licinia Sabinilla,
address this poem

to both your bodies, Artio – the woman
balancing a basketful of apples
between her knees, but also that wild creature
snuffling and whiffling

over gorse and sweetbriar, beseeching her second
self with doleful, less than human eyes to let
her taste even the worst-bruised windfalls, stolen
from some man's orchard.

Einstein's Watch

MAITREYABANDHU

Any walk I've done, such as I have done,
which isn't much, some April morning
or summer's day, has been just far enough
to find a placc to sit and think it out,
except I can't decide what thinking's for
or what the 'it' might be – love is always
somewhere in the mix or some oration
prepared to knock 'em flat. I should, I know,
have tramped the frosty fields at dawn or gone out
'botanising', naming sorrel and wild primrose,
whereas I gravitate to a seat or bench
and look myself out of looking by looking at
a lyric brook throwing up a wave
or scattering, in little wavelets, feathers,
more white feathers across the further bank.

Take this pond, for instance, its border trees,
their soon-to-be-green or rather empty branches –
empty that is apart from sidelong light
striking them sidelong all along their boughs –
at times like this (like you I'm always busy)
I imagine myself as a painter in the old mode
or rather the new made old by passing fashion.
I like to look where lapping waters meet
a grassy bank or where an oak grows up,
straight up with moss around its base and question
what it was he saw and made so much of
in shadowed earth and greenness in the water
down and down. I think – or what I'd like
to think were I not complaining in my head –
this outer world of outbuildings and birds
is but the workings of our mind, its splendour
but the splendour, if we have it, of our life.
The racket the ducks make as they land, skidding
on the muddy water, making targets,
intersecting targets, proves the world
to be exactly as it seems – gates and hedges
dripping up to Oyster Hill – and yet
this everyday pornography of fact,
this such-and-such, this now-and-then, condemns
our agency and bric-a-brac of thought
to meagre usefulness, to usefulness and want.

The ducks are lovely flyers when they fly,
their airy speed with necks full out is worth
the shock of elevation (I've got Johnson's
'sudden elevations of the mind' in mind).
But what I'd meant to say, before the quacking
started and I got myself distracted
by the real, was there's something that can't be got at,
can't be accounted for on April mornings
with lazy cloud and left-over winter chill.
Not that I'm feeling particularly elevated
myself, chewing the cud of some old business,
some indignation now the ducks have flown.

They make themselves a planet, these few ducks,
populous and watery where they live,
their view of it, communion and home,
and yet the world embraces and exceeds them
as it surely must with us – I don't mean
Milton's God looking down with mercy
or regret, but another consciousness beyond
this happenstance of sense (these seeables,
these touchables and tastes), some mystery
without a brush or two of which we go
as poor and squabbling and handsome as they.
For though the pejoratives of pond life speak
volumes for our tomfoolery and lust,
there's still this busy wildfowl congregation,
these branches struck by nearly-Easter light.

And what I say is that he saw it better,
was *there* better with his haversack and brush,
finding his way, making a little progress
in some great matter he couldn't abide to preach,
a Greek effort of thought enacted, achieved
or part achieved in tessellated patches,
as if the meaning – while the ducks return
and the water troubles itself with ripples,
out and further out (one of those minor
skirmishes we're prone to) – as if the meaning,
if only we'd look long and hard enough,
were in the *non finito* of the eye.

Weren't we drawing bison on a wall
before we strung our sentence-sounds with words?
And doesn't watching cumulus reflected
(the water chopping silvery with a breeze),
the fact that language strives towards a meaning
it is destined never to reach however much
we heap detail onto detail in our rhapsodies
of metaphor and speech – doesn't it suggest
the world is Einstein's watch in which we guess
at causes, picture cogs and inner workings
so it fits with everything we know and yet,
because we can't remove the back, will never
know for sure the world we say we're sure of?

Now the ducks have all come back, clumsily
it seems, making that contented sound
which, as they gather, rises in a crescendo
of opinions and rebukes, I've sat long enough
to tell myself there might yet be some other
explanation for late winter cohabiting
with early spring, some other-seeing beyond
the binaries, a thirdness to the world.
And what it comes back down to in the end
is that 'suddenly one has the right eyes...'
Not that I'm saying I do – no-one has them
always, this side of the fire, they come
only too rarely and go, those eyes that see

the hawthorn tree, the lead-lights on the pond,
the mallards' pantomimeish colours, see them
just as they are but more exactly, heightened

by something more. And what the painter had,
apart from headaches and neuralgia, was this,
this more often, set finely down in paint.

Vanilla Ice*

ANGELA LEIGHTON

A SOUR-FACED WOMAN passed me my ice cream. Its white dome rose, compact and crisp over the rim of the cone. I had queued half an hour for it in the gathering dusk, but the pleasure of paying with pesos for the first time made the wait worthwhile. The woman accepted my note in surly silence and returned a considerable quantity of change. I dropped it in my pocket and grasped my prize. This first transaction in the local currency had bought me this cheap, innocent pleasure, as well as a taste of being part of the crowd.

Coppelia's ice cream parlour was thronged with people in the early evening. Schoolgirls stood chattering in noisy groups, women in tight jeans ambled arm in arm, and cautious, polite lovers sat side by side in the leafy alcoves that seemed purposefully set apart for them. The lights had turned the greenery of the trees to a strange, luminous aquamarine, giving them the look of an amateur stage set. Everyone in this play had an ice cream. White, pink, green or multi-coloured, they were carried like candles in a slow, roundabout procession along the paths, a sweet blessing in the warmth of the evening. My vanilla ice was the first thing I'd bought in Havana that had not cost me the embarrassment of being treated as a foreigner. My daiquiri in the hotel, my lunch in the Bodeguita del Medio, even a small cup of coffee in the Plaza de Armas, had elicited from my hosts the rude insistence that I pay, not in pesos, but dollars, dollars. I listened to the rush-hour traffic in the streets of the Vedado beyond. Its elegant, eccentric, art nouveau houses had been turned into student hostels, nursing homes and schools. Here I was, I thought, eating ice cream at the very heart of this abandoned playground of power. It might have been just what I had come for.

The sky was already turning from a flushed pale pink to a spangled black cocktail dress of stars. The tropical day had shut like a shop, the blinds going down in less than half an hour. My ice cream was melting. I finished it quick and put the dry cone in a bin. There was plenty of time before dinner in my hotel, so I continued wandering up and down in the warm dark, watching the children play tag in another tongue, listening to the palm leaves click their tongues in the breeze, and thinking of the old long crossing of the Atlantic – a thought that filled me, suddenly, with the sad heart-distances of being far from home. Strange, I thought, how places haunt each other, double up in the mind's eye. Even as I breathed the soft warm air of this Caribbean island, I seemed to sense somewhere else at the same time – an overlay, a thin tissue of nostalgias, memories, histories, poignant yet obscure.

*

It seemed such a long way – could it be so far? – past the Teatro Garcia Lorca, its restless statues waving at the sky, past the shining dome of the Capitol, that absurd lifesize replica of the other, and into the suburbs. Soon, I thought, I'll be off the edge of my map. Already, I was far from the well-marked tourist routes with their carefully named and numbered monuments. The blank workaday streets I walked down had no name on my map, as if I had walked over the rim of the known world. There were no shops or billboards, nothing to catch the eye, only these solid square blocks of flats, grey and nameless. In the curious new quiet of midday, I even began to miss the hissing stage-whispers that had followed me round the old town: 'ssst! dólares? cambio? ssst!' like a chorus of fate dogging my steps, an ironic, debased exchange rate of words. Here there was an absolutely single-minded silence. Nothing shifted in it, nothing spoke. Where were the people, I wondered? Was everyone at work? The silence accepted the click of my footsteps and gave nothing back. I counted the blocks I had passed. Surely, I thought, increasingly nervous, I was almost there?

*

A young black policeman led me down the corridor into a tiny room. He spoke courteous, exact English and begged me to sit down. I took the chair he offered. Between us, on the table, was a heavy typewriter. Otherwise the place was bare. A high barred window caught the sun in its small grid, flinging a queer striped shadow against the wall. My companion sat down. Slowly, he rolled a sheet of paper into the skeletal Olivetti before him. Its lettering looked smudged and faded with use, the black keys gaped, showing the girders beneath, and the metal prongs, fluted like fish gills, dipped to an open hollow. The thing had a grim antediluvian air which made me smile outright. He caught my look.

'You see,' he explained, 'we have no computers.' He jabbed warily at the keys with two fingers. They jerked up on their prongs and clacked down loudly onto the paper, branding their letters into its fibre. Near the end of the line a tiny bell pinged and he returned the carriage with its silver scoop.

'If we had computers...' He waved a hand helplessly in the air. 'But Washington, you know. It is always the same.'

He shrugged. For a moment I saw the bald round dome of the cupola which I'd passed earlier in the day. Places are confusing. High above me on the bare wall, a chart in various colours explained which sirens would sound in the case of emergency: for an attack by sea, by air or by land. Any moment, it seemed, some enemy force might cross the frontier. The chart did not explain, however, what should be done.

The man had stopped typing. He asked for my name, nationality, date of birth. I started to relax. This, at least, was familiar.

'So,' he declared. 'You say you have lost something?'

I hesitated, but decided not to waste any time. 'Not exactly,' I replied. 'I have been robbed.' 'Robbed?' His eyebrows shot up. Then, with a kind of well-worn patience, he lifted his hands off the typewriter and settled them in his lap.

'Yes,' I continued. 'Someone stole my bag.'

He seemed to ponder this, then answered pointedly:

'There is no crime in Cuba. After the Revolution we eliminated all crime. Before, you know... it was different then.'

He paused. The sheer scope of the subject seemed to daunt him. He concluded briskly: 'You are perfectly safe.'

'Thank you,' I replied. 'Nonetheless, I have been robbed. Someone took my bag.'

'You are sure you did not leave it somewhere by mistake? In your hotel, perhaps? In a shop? It is possible.'

I wondered in amazement where such a shop might be. I had tried hard to find some. But apart from the bookshops in Obispo, full of Soviet texts and un-copyrighted translations, or the dollar-hungry tourist shops full of T-shirts and jeans, they seemed to have been eliminated.

'I am quite sure,' I parried. 'I saw the man who took it with my own eyes. One minute it was there, then it was gone. What's more, I'm sure he'd been following me.'

I heard again the automatic suggestive whispers that followed me everywhere, like a sexual invitation, half-compliment, half-insult, or else like a vague superstitious chant, an ever hopeful-hopeless prayer to the foreigners who carried in their bags and pockets the key to a heaven of T-shirts and jeans. We both paused to take our bearings. The sun seemed to fall in an ever more insistent *trompe-l'oeil* beside me. It looked like a foiled, de-routed angel, a vision dashed against the dead-end of the wall.

'Your bag,' he continued. 'So what was in your bag?'

This at least was straightforward.

'Absolutely everything!' I rattled off my well-practised list: 'My passport, my visa card, my driving license, my return ticket to Kingston, and all my money: some travellers' cheques and dollars.'

He looked at me in disbelief: '*Todo?* All?'

'Absolutely everything,' I corroborated emphatically. 'It was all in the bag.'

'Why were you carrying it all in the bag? That is very stupid.'

I had got him there, and rounded on him mercilessly:

'But as you say yourself, there is no crime in Cuba! I had read my guidebook, and I knew it was perfectly safe.

In any case, there was nowhere to leave documents in my hotel. I asked when I arrived and was given the same answer: 'No problem. It is quite safe.' And anyway, I thought I might need them... for identity.'

To his credit he didn't blench or hold it against me. He seemed to have infinite resources of patience in the face of awkward facts.

'So... everything,' he repeated.

'I'm afraid so. And time is rather short. I must get back to Kingston on Thursday. On Monday I return to London.'

He sighed. Then looked at me out of the corner of his eye:

'Dollars? Did you say you had dollars in your bag?'

'About eighty I think.'

There it was again. I could see it in his eye: the stumbling block, the disillusionment of history, the small insurmountable fact which threatened to bankrupt the best intentions. In the museum, I remembered, the imperial eagle lay toppled and broken, the busts of the presidents smashed on the floor and the empty Coca-Cola bottles stacked under the throne. I had laughed out loud, to the surprise of the custodians. But the street language was different. There, the well-worn conspiracies continued, and the defeated power whispered and rustled at every corner: '*Sssst! dólares?*' This was a city fought over continuously in names and symbols, and the meanings of names and symbols. The facts of its history would not lie still but twitched like dreaming dogs in the sun. They rose to the eye like that round white dome, turned out like an enormous blancmange from its mould. The same, the same – and not the same. Which city was it? Washington, Havana. *Un helado de vanilla*, *por favor*. And through it all, history's theft, nostalgia, cruelty – meanings constantly adrift from home.

Then somebody's granma named somebody's boat which somebody bought, and a handful of dollars started a revolution. '*Sssst! cambio?*' A good exchange, a brilliant bargain. And the simple fact became a marvellous fable: the boat, a memorial; the name, a story. *Granma*, they called it – somebody's granma, long since translated into a public monument, the name of a newspaper, the call of revolt. Meaning is act and myth, also – changed, exchanged, turned, returned. And my handbag, I thought, is part of it all – part of this long transaction of goods which is passed on as history, stolen or bought. What's in a bag? *Todo. Todo.*

The ancient typewriter was working noisily, its mandibles turning my answers to print. I wondered what he could find to write at such length. I had not said much. The barred, squashed sunlight on the wall had shifted and shrunk to a squinty rhombus, as if the exit had narrowed. And I was getting hungry – it must be long past midday. Meanwhile, the typewriter thwacked at the paper, imprinting its words letter by letter along the necessary grooves. The bell pinged jauntily at the end of each line. It was turning me back into the required evidence: a name, a place and a destination on paper. While somewhere in Havana, I thought with wry amusement, someone else was fixing up my passport, making a match with another face or name. The papers are simple. Through them we achieve the official status, certificates of birth, nationality, death; through them we exist.

Passingly, I remembered the woman in the bookshop,

who had caught me by the elbow two days before and began to rave about going to Miami. 'You know Miami?' she whispered conspiratorially, steering me to one side, clinging too close. 'In Miami everyone is rich, very rich, yes? Plenty of dollars. Plenty of monnay and bluejins. Me? I am going to Miami. Yes, very soon.' When I told her I was English, hoping to get away, the litany only escalated. 'Ah, Elisabetta! I 'ave a picture of Elisabetta, who is so good, yes? From a magazin. Elisabetta is like the Virgen Maria', and here she crossed herself, surreptitiously, looking over her shoulder. I tried to back away but she only clung harder, mixing up her images more wildly, desperately. 'In Miami I will meet her, the Elisabetta, yes? I am going very soon. You will take me? Yes?' At this I shuffled her off rather roughly and made my escape, thinking what strange destinations people have, the unpassported ones perhaps the strangest of all.

'Now please.'

I realised with a start that the typing had stopped and my companion was looking at me quizzically across the table.

'Where did you lose your bag? What place?'

I noticed that the euphemism had returned, but let it pass.

'In a church,' I replied.

He stared at me impassively.

'*Una iglesia?*'

'Yes.'

'You mean in the cathedral?'

'No. In another church. In the Vedado.'

'The name?'

'Ah, *that* I don't know. There was no name that I could see. And I didn't think about it at the time. It all happened so fast.'

After a pause, he observed:

'There are not many churches in Havana.'

I caught the cadence of an official phrase, something he had learned by rote from a book. The subject was evidently distasteful to him. He wrinkled up his nose as at a whiff of incense.

'I know. But this church was one of them. Santa something...' I offered, unhelpfully.

'Why were you in a church?' he enquired precisely.

'I was curious.'

'The Church in Cuba is quite free,' he remarked.

Again I detected a rulebook phrase. I decided for my own sake not to pursue the matter, or to ask why the cathedral was always locked, why I had been let in only by a back door by a muttering old crone who thought I wanted to pray.

'Yes. Well I wanted to see for myself. So when I found a notice advertising the times of mass, I decided to go in.'

The look of blankness spread like a blanket over his face. I continued undeterred:

'I slipped in at the back and put my bag on the seat. There were not many people there... mostly old women.'

He waved a hand impatiently in the air: 'Are you Catholic?'

'Well, not exactly...'

He interrupted my hesitation as a thought struck him, and he pointed out with satisfaction:

'So. A believer stole your bag.'

'Well, actually, I think it was someone from outside. In fact I'm sure. A young man followed me in. I was sitting at the back and he must have seen where I'd laid my bag, snatched it up and slipped out again. When I got to the door he'd disappeared down the street.'

'Which street?' he persisted.

I got out my map and spread it on the desk.

'It's somewhere here... off San Lázaro... one of these streets. The church is not marked. But it was here.'

He was not impressed by my reasoning.

'There is no church there,' he observed disapprovingly.

'There is no church on the map,' I snapped back. 'But it's in the street. I was in it. It has a bell tower and some steps leading up to the entrance. You go in at the side.'

I drummed my forefinger on what might have been the place on the map. But the old double meanings were stirring under it. This church had no name and no place. Its licence to exist had not been given. I thought how even the times of mass had been scrawled in pencil on a postcard on the door, invisible to any except the discerning. The reality of my handbag was dwindling fast – lost in a church, missing from a map. Church and bag seemed to be swallowing each other up in a crazy insatiable appetite for oblivion, a trick of absence, a disappearing double act. Thieves, meanwhile, multiplied.

And I realised, with unease, that all that was left of this fantasy of denial was myself. I was the thing not mapped, not official, no longer documented to exist. I was the stubborn matter that stayed where it was, the inconvenient, self-evident fact that couldn't be written out, unless... I touched the arm of my chair for comfort. Where did names end and things begin? Where did the maps stop and cities start? How easy to steal reality itself, to invent new names and obliterate others. If there was no church, then, reasonably there was no bag, no thief and no crime, and the textbooks were correct. 'We have eliminated all...' My companion shrugged and muttered in irritation as he pored over the map.

'There is no church here. You must be mistaken. Perhaps it was somewhere else?'

Suddenly I realised, with a sense of overwhelming relief, that he was as frustrated as I. The fantasy embroiled us both, along with all the other ghastly fantasies of history: sugar, slavery, Madrid, Miami, the cathedral, the Capitol. They had all laid heavy hands on our maps and minds. They had all taken the truth out of our well-meaning mouths and had left their double meanings, their bizarre replicas, on the places we knew. The same, the same – and not the same. The names could always be changed again, like any kind of money: the Cathedral of the Virgin for the Cathedral of St Christopher; the virgin Mary for the virgin Elisabetta, the Church of Santa something to no church at all, in the Freudian slips of possession and desire. And my handbag in Havana, like all the rest, slipped among maps and myths which made and erased the things that were there. Names, I thought, wander off on their own; they have their own colonial impetus and power, to steal and change, take and eliminate.

The sunlight on the wall had intensified and spread to a general glow. The bars had gone. Leaning forward in desperation, I fixed my companion in the eye and insisted:

'I *must* return to Kingston on Thursday. Please, I need a ticket, passport and visa. You *must...* write something down.'

So I too, I thought, had become an accomplice, part of the toying convenience of words, whatever they happened to say. He smiled at me, struck either by the note of desperation in my voice or, as I suspected, by a shared human exasperation at it all.

'Ok,' he answered, with a perfect drawl. 'You lost your bag – in a church perhaps or not in a church. No problem.'

*

I came out into the lovely afternoon sun clutching my letter. The light was still blindingly hot and strong. It touched everything with open hand, blessed, widespread. At a decent distance I stopped to check my precious document. It was addressed in fine, formal Spanish 'To Whomever It May Concern', and then was dated, under 1 April, 'The thirtieth anniversary of the landing of the Granma.' I was almost glad of that glamorous sub-heading to my fool's date. The rest concerned the loss, place unspecified, of my bag and all its contents, meticulously listed. It was signed and stamped. I put it lovingly into my pocket. It was what I needed: official words for acquiring other official words, in a promiscu-ous, free, cross-breeding of permissions. 'Monnay and bluejins,' I thought, 'monnay and bluejins.'

As I retraced my way through the unnamed streets I wondered about granma, who she was and where she had lived – hoping, in a sense, to return to some firm foundation of things, some solid, bare, human reality which the names had not shifted and bought, short-changed in the long lucrative markets of history. And almost before I noticed where I was, I was back on the named, familiar territory, back on my map. It wasn't really far between one reality and the other. There, in front of me, was the dome of the Capitol, gleaming in the sunlight, clear and smooth against the deep blue sky, its columns upholding something, whatever it was: a kit for democracy, imperial thumbprint, thinking's double-think. I couldn't remember who had built it or why. And my guidebook, anyhow, was also lost in the bag.

Never mind, I thought, feeling for the unchanged small change in my pocket. It was all still there, solid and tune-ful. I jingled those coins in pleasurable anticipation. Later on, I thought, I'll join the crowds in the warmth of the evening, and buy another ice cream.

NOTE
* This piece of near-reportage was written after a trip to Cuba in 1986. How much things have change since then I do not know, but I offer it as a glimpse of Castro's Cuba seen from the angle of this (hapless) visitor. Its subtitle might be 'Letter from Havana, 1986'.

Poems from *Tenderfoot*

CHRIS BECKETT

Inglizawi negn!

Sometimes he stands on the balcony in his blue pyjamas
and sees it through the eucalyptus trees

slips out when day is lapping at the dark
and stands there looking over garden gates and walls

over tin roofs clicking in their own shadows
down a track that wanders into the evening

out towards the faintly green distance of hills that is so lovely
already stirring with bats and the idea of pumas

he can hear bells and bits of conversation   someone far away
banging a nail   knows himself to be small and foreign

standing on the balcony of a big quiet house
that holds him up   holding him like a hand under his feet

but never feels unwelcome in the semi-dark...
if someone hails him from the track he will call back *Selam!*

if someone asks   *where are you from, little boy?*
he will answer proudly   *Inglizawi negn!*

he does not really know right now where English is or what
but is not troubled by the things he does not understand

while his eyes follow silhouettes of long-tailed birds
and he feels this moment stretch almost forever

Sweetheart

Yemisrach puts an arm
  around her husband
whispers *hodé!* in his ear

because here you say
  my stomach
not *my sweetheart*

and I say how on the nose
  that stomachs stand
for love here in Ethiopia

where people still admit
  how close a crop –
and with it everything

we are, masticating
  sugar-burning
walking, humming

circuitries of science
  art, philosophy –
can come to being lost...

Yemisrach wets our hands
  and towels them
then Gedilu loads up

a slip of wobbly injera
  one-handed
with egg pepper stew

hodé! he says
  as he says every day
the first mouthful is for you

Pleasures of the Feast

*Poseidon was gone on a visit to the distant Ethiopians,
the farthest outpost of mankind...to accept a sacrifice
of bulls and rams, and there he sat and enjoyed
the pleasures of the feast.*
— *Homer,* The Odyssey

No, think of them instead as our close cousins
Poseidon as the sea-god lurking in our eyes

gone to guest in Ethiopia, to taste the marrow
of the south and bring it back to Greece, untouched

so let me paint
the pleasures of the feast:

those supple wine-dark boys who harvest-dance
with three-toed pigeon girls, boys again for hawks

white-robed attendants standing like fountains
gushing icy water onto outstretched hands

fish-nimble servers balancing their trays
of whitest cottage cheese and aromatic just-killed meats

a princess roasting coffee beans
a king who booms his welcome through a horn!

and in the centre, we/Poseidon hold one pale arm
firm aboard his chariot and with the other

thrust his giant silver fork into the feast –
our close cousins howl their hunger at the door

Prayer to a Saint of Two Religions

Prayer rusts! says Alemu
whose father has a sickness of the heart
and needs a lot of help from heaven

so Alemu takes words like
  mercy   penitence
and oils them in his mouth

only when they shine like trumpets
does he blast his prayer
through St Gabriel's wings

to lift his angel high into the sky
above the perfect circle of the village church
the simple white square of the masjid

In the Lion Gardens

Old men sitting in the café by the apple trees
        can you hear me?
I am an old man too we've shrunk inside our shirts
our coffees are so strong they may outlive us

I look for Tagesse *who's he?* a boy
        who I imagined in the famine
when we both were boys Tagesse shouting at it scraping by
in it grieving and enduring it just like the meaning of his name

he must be getting on an old imagined man
        no, I did not send him
to another famine or the Eritrean war I did not forcibly
resettle him in Illubabor I could not write more suffering

        my friend!

says Tagesse and rises from a bench of smiles
        because he made it through
his being here is blessed! he comes towards me now pale eyes
and short grey hair one of the courteous old men of Ethiopia

but do I clap him on the back when I had food
        and he did not? his life and mine
his acre of the mountains worlds apart   Tagesse, sit with me
beside the cages old lions have such splendid manes!

tell me your story from the start
        not its surrendered facts
but every feeling just as you might remember it
we'll sit here for a month, a year   the apple trees won't mind

until our ears are bleeding and our hearts have stopped
        my joy in boyhood filled
a thousand fizzy bottles kicked at sadness like a mule
but now I'm liverish light-headed old stomach trying to digest

the plate of misery it missed just as your happiness
        will always be half-starved
by wants and horrors which I heaped upon you years ago

open your eyes!
you shout at me, but not unkind so I stand up again
and look at you, at me and feel that I am falling

Poems from Chios (a case of knives)

JAMIE OSBORN

Ahmed's sitting with his fist in the books.
Sixteen weeks he's been waiting, handling
the stories all of swords and fish, of
what they eat beneath the waves: dead men's
fingers, jellied eels, plastic casing
for a glass eye he found on the beach.
His mother is – where – in the pages
he holds as if they might turn to salt,
bloom into crystals, like spreading ink?
Ask what he's reading –
                              he'll break your teeth.

*

Suleiman, your breath stinks. Of smoke, of
drink. Though you've not a cent or dinar
to your name, there's money burning holes
in your hands you peer through. You ask, so
I buy you hair-gel, and you eat it,
believing in the alcohol. It
will make you handsome. The sleepless nights
will darken your lids, make your lashes
seem less long. Come on, Suleiman, I'll
buy you coffee and – though I know you
will not touch it, for your mother's sake –
we'll get stoned on pot, dance together
naked down the street. Set the textbooks
ringing – arm in ashy arm, we'll be indi-
gents, two island-hoppers with nothing
left to revel in but Marlboros.

*

Into the church, the night Haroun and
his brothers stole their sister's clothes, and
that piebald cat that slept in Omar's
tent – teased with thread from their new-won, too-
big frayed trousers, tied to a glass eye –
                    the beggarwoman tapped, cast
light, one hand full of holes. Sabrina's
family, frying fish, said they saw
shining scales through the smoke, and Mother
Mary backed on the wall, mouth open
in surprise at the parents swearing
over their children's nakedness. She,
instead, would stroke them, soft as moonlight
                         falling on their hair.

*

Ali's been a professor. His eyes –
he jokes, his pupils – narrow as he
guides each child's hand through six years, seven.
My don was literature. Now he thinks
only of counting, maps: sixteen in
1989; seventy-three,
present era...
               What is it, Ali,
that keeps you beating, waiting, and each
hand that goes up, you refuse?

*

She's learned to listen to silence. To
open the door, spread her palms: welcome.
Every morning she sits beside her
husband, counts his breaths. Every evening
she lets him enter, impassively,
irrevocable sunset. Her back
straight as a poplar, eyes closed, arms weighted
with the only promises she's kept:
marriages annulled, a boat that sank, words
she can and cannot speak. Then, she leaves,
to go to Athens. The night before
her husband at last knocked out her teeth.
Through a mouthful of dates, she smiles, says
                    it will save on dentist trips.

*

Junior's cabin is thick with the smell
of twenty stagnant men. He does press-
ups in the shade, star-jumps dazzling their
forty eyes. A beard so thick they think
God could hide in there beside his breast –
and in his arms he receives each child
the camp has borne.
               So, when his mother
washes up before, spreading her hair,
particoloured flag, he makes no sound.
Wraps her body about his own and
carries her as far as the mountains,
buries her without prayer. Watching from
the floor below, the men, motherless,
believe in him at least, make his words
signs of what they cannot bear, and miss.

*

It's worth the day off: lie on your back,
watch the ceiling turning upside down,
sunlight falling through flakes of plaster,
mould, leaves, spinning through next door's broken
window, a boastful mazurka, dark
Greek lullabies, a round you almost
join. Omar appears, his brothers with
gapped and crooked teeth. Like clouds you shred
by walking on, or the German pour-
ing backwards through their mouths, their ears, their
chests expand, until they fill the room
with Kurdish, coffee-coloured flowers.

*

They're bringing gifts: not myrrh, frankincense,
but a white towel printed grey and black
with droppings. A young Moroccan, eyes
where his mouth should be – slick, he's knocking, there's
blood on the stairs, in plumes. Headphones on,
you would ignore him, but History is
squatting by the door, damp has swelled the
frame, until it cracks. And then the shots.

Chios, July – September 2016. Brussels, January 2018

Three Poems

JENNIE FELDMAN

Lookout

God no
but a likeness or two

up there watching you
watch ribbed strays amble and pee

on old trees giving up
no man's olives

as cloud shadow
slips across quick as Elijah

on the run south
(fearful stopover

in these hills Jezebel
breathing hard in a nightmare)

bright ghosts with baskets
knowing no Wall

stooping to gather
khubeizeh's rounded leaves

How to Translate

... dull curses from the carpet seller
deadweight days rolled on one shoulder
and you not buying; life's foul luck
the muck of it, the ruck he's stuck in

... trucked-in olive trees when you ask
habibi, are you lonely, do you mind
playing traffic island, standing in
for belonging?

... mynah birds flown
free, mimicking
blackbirds they're evicting,
getting it (anyone listening?)
brazenly wrong

... what it's meant to say
forty feet up   the tree on a column
gaunt limbs
praying for heaven
knows what
(dangling water-pipes
flinch in the wind, dry olives
pelt the ground)

... the gaping sparrow full grown
on a ledge, hopping back
and forth, no song

... yellow-pink haze, chemico-
apocalyptic – what you
call sunset and ride into

Epic

Παράξενα απόψε με κοιτάζεις [...]
(from a popular Greek song)

You're looking at me strangely tonight... Slumped under fairy lights, Orestes doesn't
care. Pours more wine, adds Cola for a steady head, these being terrible times.
BATTLEPROOF says his leather jacket front and back
Dark – a catch, near-sob in her voice – *dark suspicion eats at my insides*
He looks up. The shock-red dress
it must have been her tapping the quayside. Flame parting the crowd
or a goddess feigning blindness
Let me die for you... Hands to breast and reaching out
            – To him? He sits up. Scans the locked night of her eyes
Before my golden dreams are knocked down...

On the curved brushstroke of the shore two helmeted figures – crimson, black –
riding as one. White tints for the slim, clasping arms.

That Whip of Sparks

Some Notes on Alice Oswald

ROWLAND BAGNALL

TOWARDS THE END of September, I went to see Brink Productions' adaptation of Alice Oswald's poem *Memorial* (2011) at the Barbican. It was ambitious, featuring a chorus of two hundred or so choreographed performers accompanying a minimalist orchestral arrangement, the stage at times flooded with bodies standing for the excavated Greek and Trojan soldiers of Oswald's poem, what she refers to as her 'translation of the *Iliad*'s atmosphere'. The poem itself was delivered by the Australian actor Helen Morse, whose command of the poetry I can't contest: at the very least, her recital of the poem constitutes a feat of memory of the kind I've long since given up, though there were moments of what seemed like genuine pity leaking through her voice. Nevertheless, I couldn't help feeling conscious that I wasn't hearing Oswald speak the poetry herself, that just as the American imprint of *Memorial* is subtitled a 'version' of the *Iliad*, so Morse's delivery of the poem was somehow other than the original: not worse, but not *it*.

Oswald has performed *Memorial*, several times, in its entirety, though it seems unlikely that she'll resurrect the poem anytime soon. 'It's very horrible to do,' she suggests to Max Porter in an interview for *The White Review*: 'Before I do it I have this feeling of pressure. This line of soldiers queuing up that has to move through my head. I have every muscle tensed.' Oswald's reputation as a memorable and captivating reader of her poems was all but cemented around the time of these performances. 'I saw you recite the whole poem in Edinburgh,' says Porter in the same interview, 'and – as I'm sure you're sick of hearing – it was a shattering physical and emotional experience, quite unlike anything I've ever seen.' To those, like me, who failed to witness one of these recitals, there are a handful of recordings available online (try the Hay Festival's 'Hay Player') and even a seventy-seven-minute Faber Audio CD, which Andrew Motion included in his list of 'The 10 best recordings of poets' reading their work. And yet, like Morse's version of the poem, these recordings serve only to increase my sense of having not been present at the time. As for the publications themselves, reading Oswald's poetry on the page, especially her longer pieces – I'm thinking of *Memorial*, certainly, and *Dart* (2002), but also of 'Dunt' and 'Tithonus' from *Falling Awake* (2016) – feels increasingly like coming face to face with the record of an event I failed to attend, as though the printed text of each poem amounts to a kind of visual documentation of its faded oral/aural life, at best a sort of hardened echo.

In an important sense, this frustration seems appropriate. Oswald's interest in the Homeric tradition of oral poetry is well worn, bearing heavily on the tension between her poetry as it exists in performance and as it then comes to appear in print. I'm not that interested to draw a comparison between Oswald's writing and the world of contemporary performance poetry, which I basically don't know anything about. But I am interested to suggest a view of Oswald's poetry alongside several artists to whom the importance of documentation plays a significant role in the completion and reception of their work, a way of holding back a trace of what would otherwise be lost. For Oswald, some idea of transience is integral to oral poetry, and to Homer in particular. '[The *Odyssey*] is after all an oral poem, composed in performance,' she wrote for the *Telegraph* in 2014, 'like snow, perfectly formed and ready to vanish. It is not a spatial text, but something temporal and sounded, which can only proceed as it were by melting':

> Like when god throws a star
> And everyone looks up
> To see that whip of sparks
> And then it's gone

You don't have to read much of Oswald's poetry to get a feel for her habit of tuning into other voices. The cast of *Dart* is wide, each character delivering their lines in as much time as it takes the river to wash over them. The same goes for *A Sleepwalk on the Severn* (2009), the most dramatic (and overtly Beckettian) of Oswald's books to date, whose dramatis personae cycle through the poem's nightly phases with the coming and retreating of the tide. A great many of the shorter poems crackle in and out of voices, too, often giving brief voice to the voiceless – see 'A Winged Seed' or 'Autobiography of a Stone' from *Woods etc.* (2005), or the eponymous 'Thing in the Gap-Stone Style' – all of which contribute to a general sense that voice, in Oswald's poetry, is momentary, never more than a single breath away from being lost, or cracked, or paused, or faded out, as visualised by the dissolving stanzas at the close of *Falling Awake*. Hughes's riddling 'Wodwo' certainly seems to be nosing around here, but there's a harsher side to Oswald's heteroglossia which makes me think of Beckett's *Play* (c.1963), in which three urn-bound lovers are rapidly and irregularly spotlit into action, only permitted to speak (or are they being forced?) – Beckett's stage directions use the word 'provoked' – as and when the light directs them to.

The reason for mentioning all this is to suggest that Oswald's interest in poetic voice relates importantly to her poetry in performance, to its oral lifespan, and to the relationship between her poems as they're spoken and as they turn out on the page. This isn't a new question, but it's one to which Oswald seems especially attuned. 'She instructed her audience to put away their books, as she would be speaking by heart,' wrote Claire Armistead of one of Oswald's performances in 2016: "Forget the fixed text, because I like the idea of poems being these melting ice shapes that vanish and are only there in the moment".'

*

In 1974, at the Galleria Studio Morra in Naples, Italy, the Serbian artist Marina Abramović delivered the first and only performance of her artwork, 'Rhythm 0'. 'My plan was to go to the gallery and just stand there,' she recalls in her recent memoir, *Walk Through Walls* (2016), 'behind a table containing seventy-two objects: A hammer. A saw. A feather. A fork. A bottle of perfume. A bowler hat. [...] Pins. Lipstick. Sugar. A Polaroid camera. Various other things. And a pistol, and one bullet lying next to it.' The performance lasted a total of six hours, beginning at eight p.m., during which time the audience were invited to use the objects on the artist 'as desired'. After three hours the activity escalated quickly, culminating in a scuffle as members of the audience stepped in to forcibly remove a man from the gallery for placing the loaded pistol in Abramović's hand, the barrel turned towards her neck. 'And then, at two a.m., the gallerist came and told me the six hours were up,' writes Abramović: 'I stopped staring and looked directly at the audience [...] And a strange thing happened: at this moment, the people who were still there suddenly became afraid of me. As I walked toward them, they ran out of the gallery.'

As with the majority of Abramović's performance artworks – beginning with the first of her 'Rhythm' series, 'Rhythm 10' (1973), in which she attempts to stab a sequence of kitchen knives back and forth between her outstretched fingers at speeds – 'Rhythm 10' survives only in photographs. For many, these are the only way to experience Abramović's work and (for the most part) they exist as the only remnants of – and indeed, like all photographs, go some way to emphasising – the transience that they preserve. Max Porter alludes to Abramović briefly in *The White Review* interview. 'That's something I'm more and more interested in,' replies Oswald. '[T here is still nothing like the physical fact of a human offering you something.'

Though of a very different kind, Oswald's recitals – particularly of her long-form pieces *Dart*, *Memorial* and 'Tithonus' – involve a level of endurance that reminds me of Abramović. More than this, however, I'm drawn to the idea that publications of Oswald's poetry behave in some way like the photographs left over from Abramović's performances, as though the poems on the page refer in kind to a performance that has long since been and gone. This is something that seems to guide the poetry of Sean Borodale, whose most-recent collection *Asylum* (2018) continues his practice of recording on-site compositions, part of his ongoing project to develop a poetic form he calls the *lyrigraph*, 'in which the moment of writing is an intentional performance' of which 'The text is [a] record; a transcript of [the] live experience *of* the performance of writing'.

Borodale has also written about his habit of 'writing whilst walking', whereby 'the act of walking [generates] the metabolic rate or poetic pulse of the poem-in-progress', prominent in the development of *Notes for an Atlas* (2003), a three-hundred-and-seventy-page topographical poem composed during a fifty-mile excursion around London. Imagining the poem as the real-time record of a walk-in-progress recalls the 'songlines' of Australian aboriginal communities, as documented by Bruce Chatwin in the 1980s, where the landscape is sung into existence for the duration of a given journey, the lyric description exactly corresponding to the unfolding geography, imbued with narrative significance, a kind of oral mapping process, part cartography, part creation myth. Oswald's own familiarity with the songlines is clear from *Dart* – she describes the poem as 'a songline from the source to the sea' – and she includes a translation of the aboriginal 'Song-Cycle of the Moon-Bone' in her anthology, *The Thunder Mutters* (2005). But the songlines link her thinking once more to Abramović, who spent several months with the Pintupi aboriginals in 1981, accompanied by her then artistic and romantic partner, Ulay. As Abramović recalls, learning about (and living with) the songlines played a significant role in the development of her performance art: 'You look at this landscape, and hear this story, and it's not that it happened in the past, it's not something in the future. It's happening now. It is always now. It has never 'happened.' It *is* happening. This was a revolutionary concept to me – all my ideas about existing in the present came from there.'

*

The American essayist and critic Rebecca Solnit has considered songlines, too. In *Wanderlust: A History of Walking* (2000), she uses them to illustrate a point about the connection between narrative and travelling. 'The songlines are tools of navigation across the deep desert,' she writes, 'while the landscape is a mnemonic device for remembering the stories: in other words, the story is a map, the landscape a narrative.' Later in the same book, she refers to Abramović and Ulay's piece 'The Lovers' (1988), known also as the 'Great Wall Walk'. Conceived a few years prior to its execution, the walk is primed with narrative significance. Beginning at opposite ends of the Great Wall of China, the two intended to walk towards each other – each traveling a distance of 2,500 kilometres – meeting in the middle after three months, where they planned to marry. By 1988, the three-month journey came to mark the end of their romantic and professional relationship, each step taking them closer to an inevitable separation. In addition to the usual photographs, *The Lovers* is preserved in a documentary film directed for the BBC by Murray Grigor, which shows the sad and awkward moment when Abramović and Ulay meet. Abramović is quiet, hardly speaking, her face occasionally obscured by a red flag. Eventually, she starts to cry, emotionally and physically exhausted.

In *A Field Guide to Getting Lost*, published five years after *Wanderlust* in 2005, Solnit turns her attention to 'one of the first of a new kind of photograph to become important in [the 1960s]', winding the clock back nearly thirty years from 'The Lovers' to consider the rise of photography as a means of preserving artworks that were 'too remote, too ephemeral, [or] too personal to be seen otherwise, [...] that could not be exhibited and would otherwise be lost, so the photograph stands in for [them]'. The photograph in question is Yves Klein's 'Leap into the Void'. Made in October 1960, the picture shows a quiet Parisian street, empty but for a single figure on a bicycle, seemingly oblivious to the extraordinary scene behind him: a man with tousled hair, impeccably dressed in a dark suit, leaping out across the street as if to launch himself into the air. Striking though the image is, the picture is a fake. It's actually two photographs, taken and stitched together for Klein by the photographic partners

Harry Shunk and János Kender. But Klein did leap, into a tarpaulin held taught for him by ten judokas – Klein achieved a fourth *dan* black belt on a fifteen-month trip to Japan in 1953 – cropped from the photograph in favour of an empty street. And yet, despite the forgery, for Solnit, the photograph remains 'the only trace or souvenir of the work of art, which is the leap itself.'

One way to contextualise the 'Leap into the Void' is as part of Klein's attempts to get away from the material. In a lecture delivered to the Sorbonne in 1959 he explains the development of his 'blue period', which produced perhaps the most famous and recognisable of all his works, featuring his patented International Klein Blue, a deep shade of ultramarine that came to dominate his art. Klein describes his discovery of monochromatic painting alongside the feeling 'more and more' that the predominant elements of figurative (and even abstract) painting – 'the lines [...] the contours, the forms, the perspectives', etc. – were nothing more than 'bars on the window of a prison'. 'The painter of the future will be a colorist of a kind never seen before,' he continues. 'And without doubt it is through color that I have little by little become acquainted with the Immaterial.' The 'Leap', to my mind, shows this acquaintance almost literally, Klein suspended in mid-air, surrounded by nothing, his trailing foot a hair away from lifting off. As Solnit writes of the picture, Klein leaps 'as though he need not even think of landing, [...] as though he were entering the weightless realm of space or the timeless realm of the photograph that would hold him up above the ground forever'. And so the picture is a kind of blueprint, a premature expression of the relationship between performance and documentation – between the artwork and its footprint – that would capture the imagination of Abramović and others in the early 1970s.

Several years before Klein's 'Leap', another artist had been working to preserve the image of the body 'entering the weightless realm of space'. Beginning his career as a documentary photographer on the streets of New York City in the 1930s, Aaron Siskind developed an interest in the camera's ability to transform action into abstract shape. He began to photograph the feats and twists of acrobatic divers, mid-fall, capturing their bodies in a void of empty space with the aid of a high-contrast development process. The resulting series, which Siskind added to for over a decade, is *Pleasures and Terrors of Levitation* (c.1953–65). Though I don't think Siskind ever considered his photographs to be the 'trace or souvenir', as Solnit has it, of the divers' jumps, the pictures certainly call out to Klein. I'm not sure he ever saw them, suffering a fatal heart attack – his third that year – in 1962. An image from Siskind's series, number 474, appeared on the cover of *Falling Awake* in 2016.

*

'The Era of Various Views On What One Would Have Done Had One Lived Longer', reads the final line of Anne Carson's poem 'Eras of Yves Klein', one of twenty-two individual chapbooks that make up her recent publication *Float*, also published in 2016. Running roughly chronologically, the poem imbues Klein's life and artwork with a sense of inbuilt transience. Each line presents a detail from the artist's life, some personal, some professional, no sooner offered than moved through into another stage: 'The Era of Proposing Plans for a City Built of Compressed Air Currents / The Era of Asking Aunt Rose for a Citroën / The Era of Filling Pages of One's Notebook with the Word "Humility"', etc. The whole poem reads something like a lean and trimmed biography of Klein, affectionately sending up his artistic innovations and eccentricities. It is Carson's way of holding back the artwork that was Klein himself.

Looking back through *Float* to find the Klein poem I came across an additional pamphlet of 'Performance Notes', detailing the performance particulars of nine of the collection's parts, suggesting something of Carson's own attentiveness to the relationship between performance, text and transience. One note refers to the essay 'Cassandra Float Can', a lecture in three parts, 'first presented at the Brooklyn Academy of Music in 2008, accompanied in performance by images of the works of Gordon Matta-Clark [...] carried about the room by nine to twelve volunteers'. Here's the moment from that essay where Carson turns to Matta-Clark, an architect-turned-artist from New York whose best-known work was made during the 1970s:

> Not one of GMC's artworks is extant. To know what they were like you have to consult the archival photographs or ask people who saw them. What GMC liked to do was cut things, usually big things. He split a house in half in New Jersey in 1974. [...] He made a diagonal pattern of spherical cuts up through the floors, ceilings, and roof of a Chicago apartment complex in 1978. These structures were all slated for demolition before he found them and he got permission to intervene in and alter the process of ruin. His best-known work is one for which he did not get permission. In 1975, prowling around the NYC waterfront, he found an abandoned pier that appealed to him. He broke into Pier 52 and spent two months making cuts twenty to thirty feet long and ten to eighteen inches thick in the corrugated steel of the wharf building.

The Pier 52 piece was 'Day's End'. It stood in place for two years before it was eventually demolished by the city's Economic Development Agency in 1977, a year before Matta-Clark's death from pancreatic cancer, aged thirty-five, only a year older than Klein. Like 'The Lovers', 'Day's End' is survived not only by photographs but in a film, a silent twenty-three-minute sequence showing Matta-Clark at work removing huge sections of steel and wood from the building's walls and floor. As he and his team carefully remove the largest, sail-shaped piece, the dim interior is flooded with light. It's almost too much for the camera to handle, bleaching the footage.

I haven't worked out who shot the film. It's usually attributed to Matta-Clark, despite the fact that he appears so often in the frame. While looking around for who might be responsible I came across a striking photograph, taken in 1971. It shows Matta-Clark, suspended by his ankle from the metal frame of another New York City pier building, silhouetted against a pale grey sky, his free leg bent, looking like a trussed-up outlaw, waiting to be tried, or a hanging escapologist. The photograph is part of a series, 'Parked Island Barges on the Hudson', documenting Matta-Clark at work on another project. The photographs are taken by Harry Shunk and János Kender, the same photographers who – eleven years previously – had also captured Yves Klein leaping out across the street.

Matta-Clark's incisions appear to comment on several things: on the nature of residential and commercial architectural design, on the division between interior and exterior living, on the processes of urban demolition and renewal. Above all, they are about duration, one eye fixed on their inevitable destruction. With their emphasis on endurance, Abramović and Ulay's artworks are about duration, too, carried out with the same knowledge that, at some point, every performance must come to an end. The cruelty of 'The Lovers' is that it plays this paradigm out twice, the walk referring not only to its own completion but to the end of their relationship.

The first artist to consider walking as an aesthetic act in its own right, so the story goes, was the English sculptor Richard Long. In 1967 he produced his famous photograph, 'A Line Made by Walking'. The picture shows an empty field scored by a single narrow line, the result of his walking up and down repeatedly along the same straight length of grass. As with Klein's leap, it is the walk and not the photograph which is the work of art. Over the years, Long has developed several ways to document his work, from tracing his walks back onto Ordnance Survey maps to textually recording them in a kind of concrete poem (see *DARTMOOR TIME* from 1995).

There's a lot that could be said of the relationship between Long and Oswald's work, not least about songlines, or the significance of transience, or about their shared interests in water, time, and measurement, or the reproduction of Long's 'Walking a Circle in Mist', Scotland' (1986) on the hardback cover of *The Thunder Mutters*, or even about their respective connections to Dartmoor National Park, where a great many of Long's walks have taken place.[2] But I'm not going to say that here because I don't think I've got space. Instead, I want to think about the word *trace*, as in 'the track made by the passage of any person or thing', but also the 'vestiges or marks' that indicate 'a former presence' (according to the *OED*).

The word appears often in the discussion of photography. Rebecca Solnit has already used it once in this essay, discussing 'Leap into the Void': 'the only trace or souvenir of the work of art, which is the leap itself'. It's an important word for John Berger, also, appearing in 'Uses of Photography', an essay from 1978 dedicated to Susan Sontag. Sontag's own book, *On Photography*, was published the previous year, compiled from a series of essays she had recently completed for the *New York Review of Books*. '[A] photograph is not only an image (as a painting is an image),' she writes, 'it is also a trace, something directly stencilled off the real, like a footprint or a death mask.'[3] 'A Line Made by Walking' is two traces in one: it shows a trace and *is* a trace, both at the same time. It's an important word to hold in mind when thinking about Long, or Matta-Clark, or Yves Klein, or Abramović. It's an important word for Oswald, too, who identifies in Homer's poetry a lingering trace of the real world. 'A tree in a Homer poem really is a tree - not Homer's tree, but a green, leafy, real thing,' she says to Sarah Crown in an interview from 2011: 'The puzzle I've spent my writing life trying to solve is, how does he do that?'

This may conjure Jack Spicer's lemons, but it also shares in something Oswald finds in Hughes, a way of summoning up the real, 'brought back into being in the medium of language'. 'It was a new idea to me', she writes in an article for the *Guardian* in 2005, in which she describes her early encounters with Hughes's poetry:

> that instead of describing something (which always involves a separation between you and the object) you could replay it alive in the form of sound. You could use poetry to reveal what it sounds like being outdoors: the overlapping of thousands of different noises: the rain's rhythm, the wind's rhythm in the leaves, the tunes of engines, the beat of footsteps.

For Oswald, Hughes and Homer's poetry behaves like Sontag's photographs: it is 'directly stencilled off the real, like a footprint or a death mask'. There's something about the aural quality of language - 'the form of sound', both tangible and not - inherent to this process. I wonder if it has anything to do with *enargeia*, a Greek word meaning something like 'bright unbearable reality', which governs Oswald's translations of Homer in *Memorial*:

> Like when god throws a star
> And everyone looks up
> To see that whip of sparks

*

Discussion of Oswald's poetry (as far as I can tell) has tended to focus on her position at the front of a long line of British 'Nature Poets', stretching back at least as far as the Romantics, from Wordsworth, Clare and Hardy through to Hopkins, Thomas and Ted Hughes. The hope of this essay has been to widen the lens, suggesting a parallel chain of references. Another hope - by way of the artists mentioned - has been to emphasise the importance of Oswald's poetry in performance. To ignore this aspect of her work, it seems to me, is to ignore a whole side of the coin. Returning once more to the Porter interview, Oswald is on the verge of saying this herself. 'I originally took to reading my poems out loud,' she says, 'because I found people didn't read the tunes properly on the page': 'A tune (to me) is a tension - its ending is stretched from its beginning and you can't cut it without losing that tension [...] [It's] one of the reasons I almost can't bear to put poems in books any more.'

NOTES

1 *Walk Through Walls* reveals another way Abramović's artworks are preserved. In 2007 she met the photographer Marco Anelli. Agreeing to let Anelli photograph her for the first time, Abramović arranged a brief, ten-minute photoshoot in Rome. 'He arrived exactly on time,' she writes, 'with an assistant and a great deal of camera equipment. When I asked how I should pose, he said, "I'm not interested in your face – I'm interested in your scars."'

2 It's become impossible for me to read the opening lines of *Dart*, about a solitary walker on his way to Cranmere Pool, the river's source, without thinking of Long.

3 I'm reminded of another of Klein's eras. During 'The Era of Putting a Canvas Out in the Rain', Klein was busy attempting to capture 'the spiritual mark' of 'momentary states'. Working outside he would expose blank canvases to the elements, often pressing them against various surfaces in order to 'obtain a vegetal mark'. 'Then it begins to rain, a fine spring shower,' he writes in an essay of 1960: 'I expose my canvas to the rain, and it is done. I have captured the mark of rain! The mark of an atmospheric occurrence.'

Three Poems

CAROL RUMENS

Variations for W. S. Graham

on the centenary of his birth

> *I have made myself alone now.*
> *Outside the tent endless*
> *Drifting hummock crests.*
> *Words drifting on words.*
> *The real unabstract snow.*
> *– W.S. Graham, 'Malcolm Mooney's Land'*

What everyone thinks, I
suppose, who has time
to form thought-like
shapes during the long
plunge into the crevasse;
many, all their lives,
have traipsed towards it,
equipped but unprepared
ever to hear it holler:
I have made myself alone now.

The only paradise
is motion, lost
to encampment, both
improvised. Sometimes
the bed must be unfolded
still warm from under us,
torn for another sail;
on the plate, the bleak dog-meat,
outside the tent endless
drifting hummock crests.

Bodies row their own
furrows, wry channels,
other breathers always
just out of earshot.
Now and again the mouth
makes kissing-sounds.
The pack (the pawed god
of the team) will quicken now,
mapping the maps, fresh
words drifting on words.

You know where I'm going
with this. Of course.
It's January, the coarse-
gritted wind of a hundred
Januaries hurtles
from your mound. Yr Wyddfa freckles
with treacherous blackthorn.
High-skilled for the gradient
you're gracing it through
the real unabstract snow.

A Wooden Swing

Two variations on Osip Mandelstam's
'Tolka chitat...'

I. UPSWING

To read only children's stories,
Cultivate little ideas,
And rub away the tears
Of adult categories...

Life? It's a rouble's-worth,
But here's the thing –
I want to sing and sing
My poor, rich, singular earth.

A garden, a child's swing –
I'm flying on the bare
Plank, king of the fir,
through this wild darkening.

II. DOWNSWING

Never to answer emails;
To read kind horoscopes
Only, and let the snails
Chew my envelopes...

What a waste of a good idea,
Childhood was! Light kills
Both snow and clay's career:
Why all these daffodils?

We made a swing for our hopes
On a branch long overgrown.
They've kicked the nettles down.
They jeer from weathered ropes.

To Gwynedd

'Meseems I see the high and stately mountains
Transform themselves to low dejected valleys.'
— 'Ye Goatherd Gods', Philip Sidney

Land of our grandmother, Alys Emily!
Land not entirely unambiguous
in welcome, creasy grin a kind of judgement,
you're so old you're young – wild teenager,
harddegau gwyllt [1]
your slept-in-look eternally morning-after-
the-mountain-rave, petrified evidence
of ruckus, rape and knife-fight. Slumped in riverine
spillage, they who love you
might wake up poets   if they wake up.

Strung out on bright blue lakes
we take the hairpin bends too
Jesus   too
fa   slow down! Volcano madness, this is!
They'll kick us soon as look. I hardly see them
for seeing our bones cheese-sandwiched in the landbits
we owned, whose cast-off selves owned all of it
and reasoned, 'Let the Welshman break the stone.'

Payback-seductress, summer Gwynedd fleeces
the fleecy-lined colonists from Chester
and Merseyside and Moscow with
Llanfairpwllgwyngyllgogerychwyrndrobwll-llantysiliogogogoch,[2]
with pretty inn-signs, warmish beer, sogged fries.
She drains the thirsty drop-outs from all over,
to her sale of mushroom-magic, yurty glamping,
the rock 'n' roll of waterfall and runoff.
Old music-mouth, old gossip, mocker, peace-

offering your ironic cartoon dragon
to Grendel's fossil claws,
Gwynedd, don't be angry!
Our shiny notes are bankable, at least.
Don't die to us. Let's end our letters only
as Alys Emily Davies, gifted in
the paler dragon's tongue, would temporise
in the blue shadow of her mountain ranges,
'Must close for now, dear. Yrs. Affectionately...'

1 'wild teenager'.
2 the Angelsey place-name translates as 'St Mary's church in the hollow of the
white hazel near to the fierce whirlpool of St Tysilio of the red cave'.

Poet of War

Jean Moorcroft Wilson, *Robert Graves: From Great War Poet to* Good-bye to All That, *1895–1929* (Bloomsbury), £25

GREVEL LINDOP

JEAN MOORCROFT WILSON's book, the first part of a two-volume biography, carries in its title a no doubt intentional ambiguity: great poet of war, or simply poet of the Great War? The question is not ultimately answered, but one valuable feature of this book is its decision to put the war poetry, so much of which Graves himself later suppressed, at the centre of the story. And that is by no means its sole achievement. Anyone reading this book will come away with a fresh, and deeper, understanding of Graves and his writing – even if they have read previous biographies; which, given that the last full accounts appeared almost a quarter of a century ago, is now perhaps unlikely.

Admittedly, on first hearing of Moorcroft Wilson's project, I wondered what she could possibly add to the three previous, and very substantial, lives. Martin Seymour-Smith's *Robert Graves: His Life and Work* (1982) was the work of an astute critic, who had lived with Graves and his family, and had witnessed not only the onset of Graves's dementia but those moments of searing clarity when Graves, his bearings in the present lost, lamented things he had done during the war. Miranda Seymour's *Robert Graves: Life on the Edge* (1995; the title seems meretricious until one sees how aptly it represents the way Graves lived much of his life) revealed far more about the poet's personal life: the early homosexual attachments, the way in which sex with his first wife Nancy Nicholson served as a tense, brief distraction from trauma rather than a satisfying expression of love; the weirdness of the relationship with Laura Riding – the latter available for description at last, since Riding had died in 1991. Richard Perceval Graves's three-volume life (1986, 1990, 1995) remains something of a masterpiece: stylish, imaginative and detailed, it had the advantage of being written by a member of the family who knew many of the *dramatis personae* but wasn't *too* close: the author was the poet's nephew. I shan't be discarding R.P.G.'s volumes – they remain indispensable for their range of detailed facts and dates, so shelves will just have to groan – but there is no doubt that in many ways Jean Moorcroft Wilson has outdone her predecessors.

First, and very importantly, there is her sheer knowledge of the First World War. Having previously published lives of Isaac Rosenberg, Siegfried Sassoon, Charles Hamilton Sorley and Edward Thomas, she has a military historian's grasp of the dates, geography, strategy and day-to-day details of the war, a deeply convincing familiarity with the sluggish, serpentine progress of events. We have heard plenty about 'the horrors of the trenches'; but (to take just one typical example) Moorcroft Wilson tells us, fascinatingly, that when Graves was back briefly from the front for a minor operation (a displaced septum had prevented his breathing safely in a gas mask) and sent to an army camp in Litherland, he was depressed by 'finding himself with so many of his contemporaries who were

"hobbling about... hopelessly crippled by Active Service," an aspect of war that, ironically, he forgot about in France, where people were "cleared away so soon either to hospital or under the poppies".' Safe in a boring English billet, he simply 'longed to "go home" to France'. Discussing the fine ballad 'Night March', which characteristically and infuriatingly Graves left unpublished during his lifetime, describing a twenty-three mile forced march (one stanza for every mile, she points out) Moorcroft Wilson neatly gives us the context of the night's march and makes it symptomatic of the larger predicament:

> By the time the 1st Royal Welch Fusiliers had reached their final destination in the Picardy uplands, Montagne le Fayel, 20 miles west of Amiens, they were exhausted. A journey of approximately 65 miles, which would have been a three-hour drive for the divisional general in his staff car, had taken them from 30 November to 6 December, underlining one of the less dramatic but pressing problems of the First World War again, the simple logistics of moving large groups of men and equipment even short distances.

Mention of 'Night March' reminds us that both author and reader are lucky in having access to the whole corpus of Graves's poems, so many of which he suppressed from successive *Collected* volumes: Beryl Graves and Dunstan Ward's Carcanet (afterwards Penguin) edition of the *Complete Poems* was published only in 2000 and so was unavailable to previous biographers.

It's easy to forget that Graves, regarded in the 1950s and '60s as the quintessential English poet, was by parentage half-Irish and half German. His father, Alfred Perceval Graves, was a minor figure in the Irish literary movement, a Protestant hymning the emerald isle and its picturesque stereotypes whilst beavering away as a school inspector and living in a large house at Wimbledon, relieved by spells at a similarly large holiday home in Harlech. His best-known work was 'Father O'Flynn':

> Of priests, we can offer a charmin variety
> Far renownd for learnin and piety
> Still, I'd advance ye without impropriety
> Father O'Flynn as the flower of them all

and so on. Amelie, Robert's mother, was German, great-niece of the historian Leopold von Ranke. She was Alfred's second wife; she married him after his first wife died, leaving him with five children, and proceeded to have five more of her own, Robert being third of the batch. Both Robert's parents were warm-hearted, extremely generous, deeply religious, incurable prigs and busy-bodies: qualities which Robert both inherited and fought against – a partial explanation of the contradictions in his character.

At school at Charterhouse, he seems to have been

altogether homosexual in orientation, but strongly dis-approving of any physical expression of such feelings, which he regarded as 'beastliness'. Frightened by the sexual advances of a girl, he found that, 'Boys seemed less threatening and he could allow himself to "love" one without having to face what he called at 18 "the problems, doubts and suspicions of sex".' He fell in love with a younger boy at Charterhouse, George Harcourt Vanden-Bempde-Johnstone (he appears as 'Dick' in *Goodbye to All That*) and corresponded with Edward Carpenter, but felt strongly that same-sex love was something that should be written about rather than acted upon. Graves would write early poems to Johnstone, and the relationship led to a bizarre episode when one of the masters warned Graves that their closeness was excessive and should be ended. Another boy told Graves that he had seen this master kissing Johnstone. In a jealous fury, Graves confronted the master, demanding his resignation. Johnstone confirmed the story, and the master left, to be killed the following year in France. Afterwards, Johnstone confessed that he had lied: the master had not kissed him. The real culprit was the hot-headed and intolerant Graves. Nonetheless, Johnstone remained a close friend and important source of inspiration until 1917, when he was 'arrested on Godalming Station late at night for soliciting a corporal in the Military Police, who brought charges against him'.

Graves joined the army in August 1914, just after his nineteenth birthday. Posted to France in May 1915, he was sent to the brick-stacks of Cuinchy, where a stalemate with the enemy meant that existence consisted of tedious trench-life punctuated by sniper fire. Having responded a few weeks earlier to the news of Rupert Brooke's death by telling Edward Marsh 'we can only be glad that he died... in such a good cause', he was now reflecting that, 'One can disregard a dead man. But even a miner can't make a joke that sounds like a joke over a man who takes three hours to die after the top part of his head has been taken off by a bullet.' Such experiences were interrupted, surreally, by periods of respite at the small town of Béthune, where one could get 'a really good dinner, and theatre', and drink champagne cocktails at the Café du Globe. It was during these breaks that Graves began to write some of the first realistic descriptive poetry of the war, such as 'Limbo':

> After a week spent under raining skies,
>   In horror, mud and sleeplessness, a week
> Of bursting shells, of blood and hideous cries
>   And the ever-watchful sniper: where the reek
> Of death offends the living... but poor dead
>   Can't sleep, must lie awake with the horrid sound
> That roars and whirls and rattles overhead
>   All day, all night, and jars and tears the ground...
> And then one night relief comes, and we go
>   Back into sunny cornland...

As Moorcroft Wilson makes clear, at this stage Graves had neither models nor companions in developing this new, realistic poetry. He did his best with what he could draw from Blake and Keats, as in 'The Morning Before Battle', where he depicts himself in a garden, picking roses and cherries, until:

> I looked, and ah, my wraith before me stood,
>   His head all battered in by violent blows:
> The fruit between my lips to clotted blood
>   Was transubstantiate, and the pale rose
> Smelt sickly, till it seemed through a tear-flood
>   That dead men blossomed in the garden-close.

We can sense 'La Belle Dame Sans Merci' and *Songs of Experience* behind this (and, eerily, an almost literal anticipation of the hallucinations the traumatised Graves would suffer after the war); but the struggle towards a new kind of poetry in the light of experience is palpable. Yet there was no particular programme or ideology behind this, and Graves was ready to write to some extent positively about the experience of war, as in 'A Renascence':

> White flabbiness goes brown and lean,
>   Dumpling arms are now brass bars,
> They've learned to suffer and live clean,
>   And to think below the stars.
>
> They've steeled a tender, girlish heart,
>   Tempered it with a man's pride,
> Learning to play the butcher's part,
>   Though the woman screams inside...

Their bones may whiten on battlefields, the poem concludes, 'But of their travailings and groans / Poetry is born again'. The public-school emphasis on cleanness and rebirth appealed enough to the government's Department of Information for the poem, and some others of Graves's, to be used 'for propaganda in neutral and belligerent countries'. Other poems tackled the war through allegory ('Goliath and David'), myth ('Dead Cow Farm'), as well as through grim, confrontational description – as in 'A Dead Boche' – the one war poem by Graves, Moorcroft Wilson notes, that most poetry readers can name offhand: 'A certain cure for lust of blood... a dead Boche: he scowled and stunk,... Dribbling black blood from nose and beard' – though the poem, shocking as it is, lacks an implied moral or political standpoint, relying for its effect simply on the physical repulsiveness of violent death. (Sassoon thought Graves 'wanted the war to be "even uglier than it really was"': a symptom, perhaps, of Graves's lifelong taste for the grotesque, a tinge of innate darkness which had nothing to do with the war.) Not, then, really, a great poet of war; but a necessary poet: one whose restless, tireless and sometimes inept experiments at finding an adequate medium enabled others to do greater things. Without Graves, neither Sassoon nor Owen would, probably, have achieved what they did.

Having survived Cuinchy and its snipers, Graves next went through the Battle of Loos in September and October 1915, an experience which destroyed what little faith he had in the wisdom of his commanders. Troops were sent miles on pointless errands the night before the advance; a bombardment intended to prepare the way for the infantry failed to deplete the enemy but killed a significant number of his regiment. Poison gas released by the British was caught by a change in the wind and blown back onto their own troops. Graves revised his upbeat poem, 'Big Words' ('I'll feel small sorrow... If death ends all and I must die tomorrow') by adding two crucial lines: 'But on the fire-step, waiting to attack, / He cursed, prayed, sweated, wished the proud words back.' By the end of the battle, almost half of his battalion had been killed.

Then came the Somme, where, famously, Graves was wounded and pronounced dead. A shell exploding behind him sent shrapnel through his thigh, shoulder and chest. Abandoned in a corner of the dressing-station, he was assumed dead and an officer wrote the customary condolence letter to his parents – whilst someone else noticed Graves breathing and sent him to a field hospital. Moorcroft Wilson's blow-by-blow account of the dreadful confusion in which conflicting accounts reached the Graves family is fascinating. First came a cheerful letter from Robert, minimising his injuries. Another day's post brought a second buoyant letter from Robert, a 'cautious' one from the hospital matron, and his Colonel's letter stating that Robert had died of wounds. Next was a telegram from the War Office, regretting to inform them of Robert's 'severe gunshot wound'. A further letter and telegram from Robert were succeeded by a telegram from the Army Council confirming that Robert was dead. Yet another letter from Robert was followed by a letter from his batman, confirming his death and undertaking to return his belongings, and by a wire: 'Captain Graves progressing favourably'. The death was announced in *The Times* on 3 August 1916. I wish Moorcroft Wilson had included an image of that paragraph amongst her illustrations; it would have made a fine, and ironic, parallel to the photograph (surely due in the next volume?) of Ted Hughes in 1985 unveiling a memorial tablet in Westminster Abbey to sixteen First World War poets, including Graves – who was still alive at the time.

To Graves, a natural myth maker, the Somme event became a death and resurrection: a shamanistic rite which took him out of time and history, interacting with his postwar shell-shock to create a conviction that, for him at least, normal reality was over, history at an end. His emotional history too entered a new phase. Johnston's arrest for soliciting frightened him; Moorcroft Wilson traces – though she cannot 'explain' and doesn't try to – the trajectory by which Graves became heterosexual, first falling briefly in love with a nurse at Somerville College Hospital, described as 'lively, intelligent, tall and neat', and 'almost masculine' in appearance. Next came Nancy Nicholson, artist, daughter of the better-known painter William Nicholson. A militant feminist, described by contemporaries as 'boyish', and dressed whenever possible in land girl's corduroy breeches and blouse, she must have resembled a disguised Shakespeare heroine. An unsatisfactory sex-life did not prevent the couple from having four children: intriguingly, just like his father, Robert would end up with two sets of children, almost a generation apart.

After the war, a phase of poverty, half-hearted study for Oxford degrees, and fairly undistinguished writing followed: a collection of poems beautifully titled *The Patchwork Flag* was withdrawn from publication; thin prose books about poetry and psychoanalysis (heavily influenced by W.H.R. Rivers, about whose therapeutic sessions with Graves I should have liked to learn more) were padded out with long extracts from other people's books. And then Laura Riding burst upon the scene. Poetically, Riding was just what Graves needed: her near-obsessional investigations into language and literary theory gave Graves a new philosophical focus, forcing him to look deep into the nature of both poetics and reality. Together, with *A Survey of Modernist Poetry*, they inaugurated the 'new criticism' and modern literary theory.

Riding exploded into Graves's personal life like a bomb. Rapidly separating him from Nancy and his children, she dragged him first into a bohemian couple-relationship (which seems to have worked sexually) and then into a *ménage à trois* with the Irish poet Geoffrey Phibbs. Massively intelligent and clearly paranoid, Riding had delusions of grandeur (a belief, for example, that she could 'stop T I M E') which meshed perfectly with Graves's post-apocalyptic mental state. She was also an obsessive control-freak, liable to throw herself on the floor, kicking and screaming, if she didn't get her way – Moorcroft Wilson describes her being carried out of a Rouen hotel in such a condition by waiters. When Phibbs insisted on leaving, and Riding (with Graves's obsequious support) failed to persuade him to stay, she first claimed to have drunk a fatal dose of disinfectant and then, with a final 'Good-bye, chaps!', threw herself from a fourth-storey window into the paved London basement-area some fifty feet below. Graves followed from another window, one floor down. Both survived – Graves completely unhurt, having, I suspect, run down one flight of stairs before realising that Laura would, of course, not wish him to survive her.

It takes an effort of imagination to realise that had Riding not, against all the odds, survived her very serious spinal injuries, we should now remember her as a young American poet who left a small body of remarkable poems and criticism before killing herself in London after an unsatisfactory relationship. (Perhaps mistakenly, and certainly without any prompting from this book, I found myself detecting, as I read descriptions of the young Riding in her saner days, some faint similarities to Sylvia Plath.) The book ends with Graves's hastily written but vivid and intense dismissal, not only of England and his family, but of his previous self in *Good-bye to All That*: the best and most vivid first-person account of the war, despite its many inaccuracies.

Among Moorcroft Wilson's most remarkable revelations is that an enraged Siegfried Sassoon annotated, corrected, defaced and grangerised not one, but *two* copies of *Good-bye* (one copy with help from Edmund Blunden). Sassoon, who had adored Graves, regarded his turn to heterosexuality as a 'betrayal', and resented the way Graves had derailed his attempt to protest publicly against the war by arranging for Sassoon to be treated as a shell-shock case rather than court-martialled. He was further provoked by Graves's portrayal of himself and his spiritualist mother in the book, and by the unauthorised inclusion of one of his verse letters. Sassoon persuaded the publisher to cancel several pages of text; his own countless emendations range from pedantic correction of dates to marginal annotations of 'rot', 'fiction' and 'faked', and thence to printed subheadings, pasted in: for example, 'Mummy's Bedtime Story Book' inserted below the title.

The book ends with Graves and Riding newly arrived in Majorca; *I, Claudius*, *The White Goddess* and much of Graves's finest poetry lie ahead. Jean Moorcroft Wilson's account so far has been lucid and gripping. I can't wait to read the second volume of this astonishing life. And after that, who's next? Rupert Brooke? Ivor Gurney? Gurney, for my money. Now there's a *really* great poet of war.

Sang Froid

MARGO BERDESHEVSKY

Once a year for short-lived single nights, the cereus.
These are the last days of Europe as we know it.

Morning's prowl to one of the old
four-graces-caryatids

once summer-green now stain-rot footed
by that other season's weather

here's water to quaff and bathe
a hive of city bees,

thirsty as we all are for
a more fountained life.
The West, as we knew it.

Finding it, they swig, finding them
I mourn – there are ways still
to not yet die of thirsts. All our thirsts.

(Once a year for short-lived single nights, the cereus.
These are the last days of Europe as we know it.)

Butterflies, a day.
Naked all night, no kiss.

An eclipse has an hour. Two.
A red sang-froid moon.

On an island the white sound of night,
blooming. In the south the many-voiced cicadas
drone. My motherland has no voice. Couldn't
sing. Didn't teach me.

I don't know whose one
name is 'they'.

I know they have killed the live oak.
Caged the babies.
Slaughtered the free like goats.

A girl in eyelet white. Failing in darkness. Wants
to sail in a garden pond. Falls in. Cannot breathe.

This morning's first-light finds me
finding one of history's old carved graces
 – upholding water.

Their summer-green bodies rotted with
weather where gilt bees swarm their ankles.

Where water threads spill, and they quaff,
hive-thirsty as we all are for a more
fountained life. Where finding it, they drink.

Exile: Part II

ANDRÉ NAFFIS-SAHELY

THE WORLD the Desert Fathers and Mothers had known would be forever changed by the early Muslim conquests of the seventh century, and not long after Tariq ibn Ziyad (670–719) conquered the rock that now bears his name, the notion of exile would be again revisited by Abd al-Rahman I (731–788 ACE), an Umayyad Prince from Syria, with whom the rich tradition of exilic writing in Spain arguably begins. Among the sole high-ranking survivors of the Abbasid slaughter of the Umayyads in 750, Abd al-Rahman spent several years roaming the cities of North Africa, before amassing a small army, landing in al-Andalus and conquering Córdoba, which he made his capital, much to the chagrin of the Abbasid ruler in Baghdad, who reigned, if only nominally, as caliph over the entire Muslim world. Abd al-Rahman's most famous poem, or rather the most famous poem attributed to him, is 'The Palm Tree', which takes as its subject a tree that like the new Emir of Córdoba, has 'sprung from soil' in which he is a 'stranger', becoming a memento of Abd al-Rahman's lost homeland in Syria, now ruled by his enemies.

Although Islam expanded its territory rapidly in the first three centuries of its existence, it would not ultimately retain many of its furthest outposts. While al-Andalus – or Muslim Spain – would last roughly from 711 to the fall of Granada in 1491, *Siqilliyat*, or the Emirate of Sicily, proved even more short lived (831–1091 ACE). This might explain why, in the words of the Italian writer Giuseppe Quatriglio (1922–2017), many of the works of the Siculo-Arab poets we know are imbued with 'the pain of eternal exile from Sicily'. Ibn Hamdis (1056–1133 ACE) was born halfway through the Norman conquest of southern Italy and after the fall of Syracuse, he relocated to Sfax in North Africa, before eventually making his way to al-Andalus, drawn by the reputation of its rulers as indefatigable patrons of the arts. It was during this period of exile al-Andalus that Ibn Hamdis's Sicily finally fell to the Norman invaders for good. In one of the most complete fragments of his work still extant, Ibn Hamdis imagines *Siqilliyat* as a lost 'paradise' the land of his 'youth's mad joys' which has now become a 'desert' he cannot bring him to 'bear witness to it'.

During the Tang Dynasty (620–905 ACE) in China, exile was likely the most popular of the *five punishments*, which included death by decapitation, a long sentence of hard labour, or a beating with either a thin or a thick rod, compared to which banishment to remote, barbarous regions of the Empire seemed like a far easier choice. Much like Ovid, the poet Bai Juyi (772–846 ACE) got himself in trouble at the Tang court over some controversial poems, which as he explains in his preface to his poem, 'The Song of the Lute', led him being 'demoted to deputy-governor and exiled to Jiujiang.'. The poem begins as Bai Juyi sees a friend off at the river, at which point he hears the sound of a lute being played by a woman, and since finding refined music in distant provinces was uncommon, it reminds him of his old life in the sophisticated capital. With echoes of the interactions between Scheherazade and Shahryar in *The Thousand and One Nights*, Bai Juyi begins to ask the female musicians a series of questions about her life, to which she answers: 'My brother was drafted and my Madam died. / An evening passed, and when morning came my beauty was gone. / My door became desolate and horses seldom came, / and as I was getting old I married a merchant. / My merchant cared more about profit than being with me. / A month ago he went to Fuliang to buy tea'. Although the source of their loneliness is different, they 'both are exiled to the edge of this world', brought together by the sound of music, which is minutely described throughout the course of Bai Juy's poem.

While the Tang dynasty's central government banished unpopular officials, the power to exile even the city's most influential citizens lay in the hands of Florence's masses, perhaps truly earning the city's sobriquet as the 'Athens of the Middle Ages'. Failed wars, economic instability and unpopularity could easily get Florence's leaders exiled from their own city. In fact, a spell in exile caused by one's political allegiances occurred so often in Renaissance Italy that one had to have a sense of humour about it, as Niccolò Machiavelli (1469–1527 ACE) clearly did. In his *Florentine Histories*, Machiavelli gives us an anecdote involving two of the city's most famous sons, Rinaldo degli Albizzi (1370–1442) and Cosimo de' Medici (1389–1464), the patriarchs of two of Florence's most powerful families, who played an exilic game of cat and mouse with one another for much of their lives. 'In 1435,' Machiavelli tells us, 'while Rinaldo degli Albizzi was in exile from Florence and scheming to start a war against the Florentines in the hope of returning home and chasing out Cosimo de Medici, he sent this message to Medici: 'The hen is hatching her eggs.' Cosimo's reply was: 'Tell him she'll have a hard time hatching them outside the nest.' Indeed, it was Cosimo the Elder who had the final laugh, given that Rinaldo's plot to have Florence invaded by Filippo Maria Visconti, the Duke of Milan, came to naught and he never saw his native city again.

Long before Machiavelli's time, Dante Alighieri (1265–1321), another great Florentine, was chased out of his city, an episode we can perhaps draw most meaning from by reading a few cantos situated roughly halfway through his *Paradiso*. Although Dante's journey through hell, purgatory and heaven throughout the *Divine Comedy* is studded with characters who appear incapable of speaking in anything but riddles, the poet is finally met by one of his ancestors, Cacciaguida, a warrior who was knighted during the Second Crusade (1147–1149), and who unlike anyone else in Dante's epic, does not mince his words. Cacciaguida tells Dante that his beloved Florence has been corrupted. Once a sturdy, honourable republic, its institutions have been polluted by the internecine warfare caused by greedy, competing clans – like the Albizzi and the Medici – whose plots and schemes undermined the city's government to the detriment of its citizens's welfare. Before long,

Cacciaguida warns his descendent that his own banishment won't be long in coming: 'So you are destined to depart from Florence.' he tells him, 'You shall leave everything most dearly loved' and, 'You shall discover how salty is the savor / Of someone else's bread.' Of course, luckily for Alighieri, this is paradise, where hope reigns supreme, and Cacciaguida tells his descendent that those who have exiled him will eventually be exiled themselves.

Some, of course, are fated to be exiled before they are even born and the Byzantine poet Michael Marullus (1453–1500) was certainly one of them. Marullus was still inside his mother's womb as Constantine XI Palaiologos (1405–1453) led the last desperate effort to keep the walls of the old imperial capital of Constantinople from being breached. An aristocrat with links to the former ruling family, Marullus came of age amidst the ashes of the Byzantine world, which had endured for a thousand years after the end of the Roman Empire in the West. Growing up in the maritime Republic of Ragusa, an old Venetian vassal state, Marullus later moved to Italy, where he spent periods of time in Ancona, Padua, Venice and Naples. Aged seventeen, he took up arms as a mercenary, and headed off to fight the Ottomans in the Black Sea region, but upon his return to Italy years later, he began to write poetry and forged a number of friendships with some of the peninsula's most distinguished inhabitants, including Pico della Mirandola and Sandro Botticelli, who painted his portrait. Regardless of where his dromomania led him, however, Marullus always betrayed his true roots by signing each poem with the word *Constantinopolitanus*.

There is no better statement of this exiled Greek poet's life and ideas than his *De Exilio Suo – On His Own Exile* – an intensely self-conscious lyric, apparently written while Marullus was serving as a mercenary, contains some hard truth about life away from one's homeland: 'True, all dignity of birth and family is cast off / As soon as you step on foreign land an exile. / Nobility and virtuous lineage, a house which gleams / With ancient honours – these are no help now.' Although Marullus acknowledges the loss of his world, he is obsessed with the war-like spirit he believes is necessary in order to reconquer it, a sentiment which shows its pagan roots in the line: 'Liberty cannot be preserved except by our native Mars.' Centuries ahead of his time – his belief in the need for violent rebellion would be proved right by the Greek War of Independence (1821–1829) three centuries later – Marullus was nevertheless born astride two ages, although one could safely say that his death was squarely medieval. Attempting to cross the Cecina river atop his horse, Marullus drowned at the age of thirty-seven, with a copy of Lucretius's *De rerum natura* stuffed in his pocket. Although praised by Pierre de Ronsard (1524–1585), Michael Marullus's poems may well have been lost to us had it not been for the efforts of the Italian philosopher Benedetto Croce (1866–1952), who translated his poems into Italian in 1938, a fortunate turn given that Marullus's books hadn't been reprinted since the sixteenth century.

While the troubadours in Europe sang their lyrics to eager audiences, the poems constituting the Swahili epic *The Song of Liyongo* were being recited by the troubadours' African counterparts up and down the eastern coast of the continent. Fumo Liyongo, a mythical figure shrouded in mystery, was born sometime around the eleventh or twelfth centuries, and as the story goes, although he was the eldest son of a king, he was denied his rightful place on the throne over the fact his mother wasn't the king's first wife. In these details, we can discern the great societal transformations that might have led to the composition of this cycle of poems. When Islam spread south of Arabia and into Somalia, before progressing further down the coast, the typically matriarchal society of the Bantu was supplanted by Islamic patriarchy, and thus severed from his destiny, Liyongo became a thief, who like his English counterpart Robin Hood, stole from the rich and gave to the poor. As was the case with Rama in the *Ramayana*, Liyongo's time in exile helps him hone his leadership abilities, but unlike the Indian god, Liyongo is not fated to rule. Exhibiting traits similar to many Greek heroes – among them Herculean strength – Liyongo continually evades his enemies, but is eventually killed by his own son, who plunges a copper needle into his stomach, his Achilles' heel.

*

With new kings come new laws, and 1607 struck the death knell for Gaelic Ireland. On that year, the Earls of Tyrconnel and Tyrone fled to the continent to seek Spanish aid against their new English overlord, James I. The earls had been stripped of much of their lands under the new freehold system as the Stuart monarchy paved the path for the subsequent Plantation of Ulster. It was, by all accounts, a tragic loss, leaving Ireland rudderless at a critical juncture when the tide against foreign domination might have been turned. Eoghan Ruadh Mac an-Bhaird's (c.1570–c.1630) lament in his poem 'The Flight of the Earls' begins with the memorable line '*Anocht is uaigneach Éire / This night sees Éire desolate*', before ending with the exact moment the Irish lords depart their beloved Ireland with the hope of returning as conquering heroes: 'Her chiefs are gone. There's none to bear / Her cross or lift her from despair; / The grieving lords take ship. With these / Our very souls pass overseas.' Of course, the Stuarts themselves would be supplanted in their turn. Ironically, the fate of the Irish earls would play out again in the shape of Bonnie Prince Charlie's (1720–1788) escape to the Isle of Skye after the Battle of Culloden in 1745.

*

As the world grew smaller, the possibility of soldiers and mercenaries finding themselves further from home than they could have possibly imagined became an everyday reality. Among the many anecdotes assembled and published by Percy Sholto (1868–1920), brother of Lord Alfred Douglas, Oscar Wilde's lover, we find the story of Richard Grace (c.1612–1691), an Irish Royalist who fought for the last three Stuart kings of England. When his first monarch, Charles I, lost his head, Grace was labelled a fugitive criminal by Cromwell's Commonwealth, which may have contribute to Grace's decision to serve under other governments in continental Europe, first Spain's, then France's, yet whomsoever wished to gain Richard Grace's loyalty had to consent to a chief condition: 'that they should be permitted to go and serve their own king, whenever his affairs required their service', their own king of course being Charles II.

While kings, princes and petty potentates rose and fell across Europe, in 1798 the Polish-Lithuanian Commonwealth, Europe's largest nation, was dissolved and partitioned between Austria, Russia and Prussia, unleashing a wave of Polish emigration that would last for decades. Indeed, long before the famous Légion étrangère was founded, France dispatched the Polish Legion to Haiti. Assembled by Napoléon Bonaparte (1769–1821) from captured Austrian regiments composed of conscripted Poles, eager to turn on their new oppressors, the Polish Legion were dispatched by the French Emperor to put down the rebellion in the cane-sugar paradise of Saint-Domingue. Setting off from Italy, the Legion reached the island we now know as Haiti in January 1802, carrying with it thousands of men, among them Władysław Franciszek Jabłonowski (1769–1802), an officer of mixed Polish and African heritage. Nevertheless, surrounded by a British blockade, plagued by illnesses and starved of supplies, the Legion proved unable to hold back the tide against Toussaint Louverture (1743–1803). Missives from these Polish soldiers of misfortune spell out the horrifyingly extent of their mission's blunder: 'I cannot forgive myself the naivety and stupidity that drove me to seek my fortune in America.' As Józef Zador's letter home to a friend confesses, 'I do not wish such a fate on my worst enemy. It is better to beg for bread in Europe than to seek one's fortune here, amid a thousand diseases [...]'. Those who didn't die or flee back to France, eventually switched sides and joined the rebels, becoming the ancestors of a community of Polish Haitians, who claim direct descent from Napoleon's soldiers.

The literature of travel and exploration during the early modern period in the West is largely a blood-soaked chronicle of jingoism overseas, where animalistic natives are either exterminated or 'civillised', or both. As outsider perspectives on the West during this period are quite rare, it is particularly interesting to pause on the reflections of Mirza Sheikh I'tesamuddin (c.1730–c.1800), who embarked on a diplomatic mission to Britain on behalf of the Mogul Emperor in 1765. I'tesamuddin's memoirs of his trip, *The Wonders Of Vilayet*, sees him tour many parts of the world, including a visit to Oxford's renowned 'madrassah', and his observations of the age old Anglo-French dispute are engrossing for their deviation from white masochistic accounts of the 'other': '

> The French say that the present excellence of the English in the arts and sciences, trade and industry, is the result of French education; in the past, when they lacked this education, they were ignorant like the mass of Indians. However, even the French admit that the English have always been outstanding soldiers. The French say that the lower classes of Englishmen do not go to foreign countries to seek trade or employment because, being stupid and without any skills or business acumen, they would fail to earn a decent livelihood. The French, on the other hand, are skilled in all the arts and sciences, and wherever they go they are cordially received and acquire dignity and honour in diverse professions. I realised clearly that the French are a conceited race, whose conversation was always an attempt to display their own superiority and to unfairly belittle other nations.'

It is in earlier chapters of *The Wonders of Vilayet*, however, that we come across fine description of the slaveocracy of French Mauritius (1715–1810), where the *Code Noir*[1] ruled supreme: 'The French notables live in mansions built on stockaded plots of a couple of bighas in the middle of their estates, which are cultivated with the help of a hundred or so male and female slaves. Oranges, Indian corn and vegetables are grown for the market. One half of the proceeds goes to the landlord, the other half is divided among the slaves. These slaves are brought as adolescents from Bengal, Malabar, the Deccan and other regions and sold for fifty to sixty rupees each. [...] It is reported that the Portuguese were the island's first colonisers, but they found it so heavily infested with snakes, serpents, scorpions and other noxious creatures that they were soon forced to abandon it. After them the French moved in and had better luck. French priests using a kind of necromancy caught the dangerous creatures, took them out to sea and drowned them. Since then there is no sign of them on the island. Of course Allah alone knows how far the story is true.'

It is to Dante's first American translator, the poet Henry Wadsworth Longfellow (1807–1882) to whom we owe one of the earliest popular chronicles of the first recorded large-scale acts of wholesale ethnic expulsion: that of *Le Grand Dérangement*. Also known as the expulsion of the Acadians, the term describes the British decision to deport 15,000 French colonists from their homes in Acadia (the modern Canadian Maritimes) and to ship them back to France, from where they were then resettled in Louisiana, becoming what we now call the Cajuns. Longfellow's *Evangeline, A Tale of Acadie* (1847) describes Evangeline Bellefontaine's efforts to find her beau Gabriel after the expulsion, no mean a task given the circumstances: 'Scattered were they, like flakes of snow, when the wind from the northeast / Strikes aslant through the fogs that darken the Banks of Newfoundland. / Friendless, homeless, hopeless, they wandered from city to city, / From the cold lakes of the North to sultry Southern savannas, – / From the bleak shores of the sea to the lands where the Father of Waters / Seizes the hills in his hands, and drags them down to the ocean.' The techniques behind the expulsion of the Acadians would be repeated often in future chapters of American history, including the exile of the pro-British Iroquois to Canada, the Indian Removal of the 1830s, or the Long Walk of the Navajo in 1864. Luci Tapahonso's (1953–) poem, records the forced march of the Navajos to Bosque Redondo, where, as the poet notes in her preface, 'they were held for four years until the US government declared the assimilation attempt a failure. More than 2,500 died of smallpox and other illnesses, depression, severe weather conditions, and starvation.' As Tapahonso writes: 'My aunt always started the story saying, 'You are here / because of what happened to your great-grandmother long ago.' // They began rounding up the people in the fall. / Some were lured into surrendering by offers of food, clothes, / and livestock. So many of us were starving and suffering / that year because the bilagáana[2] kept attacking us. / Kit Carson and his army had burned all the fields, / and they killed our sheep right in front of us.'

---

1 Legal code regulating both the slave trade and the conducts of blacks, slaves or freedmen.
2 Navajo for Anglos.

Four Poems

LUKE THOMPSON

Three Poems *after* Lafcadio Hearn's 'Insect Musicians'

'Let us go insect-hunting tonight,' the poet said.
'It will be dark and I have many lanterns ready.'

do not
leave the city

cicadas and crickets
in bamboo cages

                                     on a spring night
                                     Kiriyama hears

eating melon rind   still, small voices
singing about melon   risen from clay

                                     a ghost-song in the jar
                                     where our parents died

          and at my funeral
          the cage will open

          but instead of insects
          lizards and birds
          singing

'My Speech is now Decay'd'*

'I don't know how you're doing it,'
you say, believing this is all a simulation of home.
'If this is really real, go out to the garden,
where I can see you, and cut me
the flower from the top of that tree.'

I wave at you through the window,
climb the tree and cut the flower.
'I don't know how you're doing it.'

You say: 'Ali's up the artificial tree eating an unctuous pear.'
You say: 'There are ducks bigger than me out there.'
You say: 'It would be a good place to fix up the radio. The original one from years back. In the
squirrels' house where it used to be. It has transmitter *and* receiver now.'
You say: 'There are more shadows in the room today.'

Fragments of exotic birds
crowd the hospital feeder,
parrots and parakeets.

* The title is a line from Robert Herrick's 'Litany to the Holy Spirit'.

Walking the Tightrope

Philip Larkin: Letters Home, 1936–1977, ed. James Booth (Faber) £40

Reviewed by JOE CARRICK-VARTY

Larkin once said of his poems, 'I treat them like a music-hall bill: you know, contrast, difference in length, the comic, the Irish tenor, bring on the girls'. Larkin's long-awaited *Letters Home* feels very much like a book constructed in this light, and reads, rather inexplicably, like a body of work shaped and crafted by Larkin to be read as, you guessed it, a book, of poems even, not merely a collection of letters.

Letters Home comprises some 607 letters and postcards, 475 of which are from Philip to his mother, Eva, whom he affectionately calls: 'My dear old creature', and to whom he writes daily, even twice daily during certain periods of his life. These letters chart Larkin's most intimate and longstanding relationship. And they are unlike any other collection of letters I have ever read. As the sheer volume of correspondence suggests, this trawling catalogue records every conceivable chapter of Larkin's life: from university, to a first tentative mention of librarianship by his father, Sydney: 'As regards the School of Librarianship, I suppose that is the thing to do, if you contemplate making a permanent thing of that profession', to the morning his second novel, *A Girl in Winter*, was glowingly reviewed in the *Sunday Times*: 'Well, I began to read it, but it was so marvellous that I had great difficulty in reading to the end.'

But *Letters Home* also vitally recounts many important moments in British history. Larkin's first letter to his parents ('Mop' and 'Pop') upon arriving at St John's College, Oxford, in 1940 is a time capsule of student life during the Second World War: 'Very queer to hear the noise of a 'plane at night, & look out to see a moving light in the sky.' An eighteen-year-old Larkin describes all the awkward things I did during my fresher's week in 2013: buying decorations for the flat, attending ghastly meet-and-greets, locating milk: 'we scoured Oxford for milk & managed to make some tea', eating terribly: 'Yesterday we had 'grilled herrings'. They tasted simply awful: as if all the fishwives and fishmongers in Billingsgate had contributed a gob of spittle to their glutinous horror.' Some things never change.

Collections of letters have always troubled me. I'm hesitant to pick them up because sure enough I can never put the damn things down. In the same way a book of poems relies very little on linearity or narrative context, one can dive right into a book of letters, at any page, and find a satisfyingly self-contained chunk of writing, and this is rather exciting.

The idea troubles me for two reasons: 1) Letters are almost always addressed to a single person, from a single person. They are private; 2) Collected letters of poets, artists, politicians etc. are almost always published posthumously, administered en masse to the masses with little or no context and without their conceiver's consent. They are the last thing to happen to a writer. They are the final 'scoop', if you like, and for this, the transaction between reader and author feels strange. On 10 March 1963, when Larkin writes, 'It is rather a crushed creature that writes today... the sense of life being a bit too much is constantly at my elbow', I found myself asking: Should I be reading this? Why am I reading this? Alongside his 'graveyard humour', Larkin's depression is a theme which persists and persists in stark veracity throughout his letters. A theme which, while it inhabits his poems, manifests in a completely different way.

Larkin was a great cataloguer of his work, a great date-keeper; nearly all of his poems are dated. Despite my ethical quandary, there is a certain thrill to opening both his *Collected*, and his *Letters* simultaneously, finding your favourite poems, finding the date they were conceived, and then marrying them to letters he wrote during that time. 'Toads Revisited', one of my favourite poems, with that breath-taking final arrest: 'Give me your arm, old toad; / Help me down Cemetery Road' was written in October 1962. On 7 October 1962, Larkin wrote a short letter to his mother in which he discussed: 'John Cowpers's ninetieth birthday! Just think of it!... It is marvellous, isn't it, considering how ill he used to be... I believe what counts is the will to live, the basic psychic energy that you have & I haven't.' This is some reveal. Afterwards, Larkin reverts to type, to formalities and daily routine: 'I have ordered all his books for the library... There is a poem by me in *The Spectator* this week, about advertisements – not a very good one.' He's at it again: walking that tightrope between morbid humour and actual morbidity. He signs off with 'how are your roses?' It's as if he'd never mentioned 'the will to live', or his having lost it. And that's without even noting the delightful doodle that accompanies this letter and so many others. Scribbled whiskered characters acting out the letter's message, taking the place of words. Larkin's doodles are a rare gift, and deserve a book of their own.

After spending a month with *Letters Home* I realised letters are not poems. And poems are not letters. Sure, this great brick of a book will prove vital reading for any Larkin enthusiast. But what's inside is to be handled with care. Larkin's letters are not hard like many of his poems, they are not impenetrable like his public persona; they were not written for us to read.

Muffled Tumult

Song of Stars, Guus Luitjers, tr.
Marian De Vooght; *Les Chambres*,
Louis Aragon, tr. John Manson

Reviewed by JAMIE OSBORN

'All memory is individual, unreproducible – it dies with each person. What is called collective memory is not a remembering but a stipulating.' Susan Sontag was writing, specifically, about visual representations of human suffering, presented to us as testament and evidence; there is no such record of the life of the subject of *Song of Stars*, eleven-year-old Sientje Abram. She was killed in Auschwitz in 1942; Guus Luitjers's long poem is an attempt to reconstruct the events leading to her murder, oscillating between memory and stipulation. The poem is arranged in ten sections each split between Luitjers's voice and that of Sientje, with Luitjers progressively taking over until a final section lists the names of the three hundred and thirty-one children deported from Rapensburgerstraat, Amsterdam, Sientje among them.

The translator Marian De Vooght describes Sientje, as portrayed in the poem, as 'a chatterbox, filled to the brim with life, but growing quieter as her city changes'. Initially, Sientje offers anecdotes about her games and daily activity, mixed with frank confusion about 'what Jews are' and the meaning of her mother's Yiddish as much as her teacher's sudden anger; by the time of her deportation her tone is made harder, more certain:

> They write it all down who you
> are where you're from when
> you were born what do they
> care they stay here

Nevertheless, even early on in the poem, Sientje, or the poem that poses as her voice, has an acute sense of the uncanny, set in a house where 'a silent clock // knits with my mother'. Luitjers and De Vooght are well tuned to the intelligence of Sientje's observational monologues, though at times the portentousness can seem heavy-handed.

This portentousness is perhaps deliberate, as a sign of the poem's conscious engagement with itself as text. Luitjers's and Sientje's voices are framed in the same erratically sing-song four-line, three-line stanza arrangement, with echoes between them. Line breaks are carefully awkward, the stream of text unpunctuated, so that the poem is posed at once as verbatim and as artifice. Sientje has a ghostly other self – 'In my mirror my mirror / image looks at me she's called ǝſʇuǝıS' – and Luitjers asks repeatedly whether she even ever existed. Nevertheless, he addresses her:

> *Those who could forget you*
> *are murdered too so you keep*
> *on living without knowing*

Knowledge is the prerogative of the author, the researcher, but, when it comes to imagining the lives of those 'who never existed [...] filling streets restaurants', the limits of that knowledge are revealed:

> *I know the date and the hour*
> *that the train started moving*
> *all the passengers I know them by*
> *name I know their place of*
>
> *birth and where they lived but*
> *who they were I do not know*
> *and cannot forget*

To forget can also be a stipulating, in the service of nationalism and its extremes. There are troubling resemblances between the author and the enforcers of atrocity in *Song of Stars*, but Luitjers's willingness to walk the streets where the forgotten lived and '*give meaning to the signs / they left behind*' makes the difference. His deliberate poetry is an act of resistance in increasingly fascist times.

Les Chambres was the last book of poetry published by Louis Aragon, in 1969, when he had already been nominated for the Nobel Prize five times and his reputation established as a giant of twentieth-century French literature. It is partly a long love poem dedicated to his wife Elsa Triolet, by turns surreal, filmic and Rilkean in its influences and its 'long oblique ceremonial of loving', and can be read as an autobiography of the most oblique kind. It covers Triolet and Aragon's time in the French Resistance and as Communist organisers as well as their art and their aging; unlike *Song of Stars*, it has no clear narrative. More directly, it is an extravagant lament for lost time, filling the rooms of the poet's past with 'this disorder derisively called memory' and bemoaning the poet's fate in life and approaching death:

> To whom leave [sic] my legacy a cyanide
> Of failed words utopias
> Everything will always have been more bitter than the worst
>   kick to a dog
> How long it takes to die a whole lifetime

John Manson's translation largely cleaves to the word order of the French and its literal meanings, heightening the strangeness of Aragon's lyricism, at its best, its lack of restraint at its worst. The poem is saturated with anxiety about how presence may be inscribed and received, the lovers unravelling '[o]n the wrinkles of the linen written like a secret sleep of crayfish', and text is made manifest often to the point of paranoia. In addressing 'the one I have loved all my life in the guise of murder', Aragon turns the act of writing into 'muffled tumult'. If Aragon is aware of this, and despite his reflecting of 'this love of us living this love / Of us two', another kind of boast, he is more concerned with celebrating his own elaborate imagery and (gendered) art than with questioning it. 'I make / A show only of my soul', he declares. Humility is not a characteristic of the poem; Aragon perhaps says more than he means in admitting that 'Everything / Will have lost the meaning it had for me alone'.

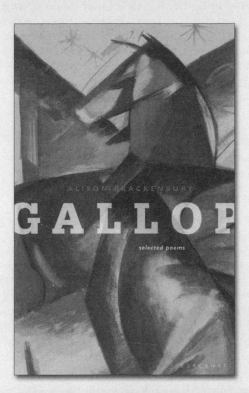

Love and Making

Emily Grosholz, *The Stars of Earth*
(Word Galaxy Press) £28.95

Reviewed by DAVID C. WARD

It's an effective tactic in an argument or an important meeting to pitch your voice lower. Don't compete with the noise but change the terms by going quieter, forcing people to listen – and perhaps reflect. More widely, in these clamorous times, reticence and restraint model a way through the noise, another way of speaking that contains the possibility of remaking or adapting traditional values for modern (or postmodern) times. Even in the small ambit of Poetry World, there seems always to be a buzz of self-promotion and attention seeking that accompanies the work itself and sometimes even blocks it. The signal-to-noise ratio is much less than it is in politics or sports but nonetheless it's still there in the literary world as a kind of background tinnitus that occasionally rises to the level of deafening. Poets, of course, are no strangers to drama but sometimes the scene stealing can get distracting or exasperating.

The American poet Emily Grosholz has crafted a career that seems unaffected by literary fashion or even current events. Perhaps because her 'major' occupation is that of philosophy professor she is freed to do what she wants in her 'minor' career as a poet. (Another poet I admire, John Koethe is also a philosophy professor and his poetry has a liberating facility to it that I find temperamentally similar to Grosholz's even though they are stylistically different.) Poetry as an avocation can be liberating, or at least it seems to be for Grosholz given the quality and quantity of the verse collected in *The Stars of Earth*. Grosholz's strategy seems to be to write poems as a commentary or literary counterpoint on the dailiness of her life. There's something admirable, I think anyway, about the ability to engage small themes in interesting ways – from 'Morning Delivery of *The Times*':

> I went out to look for the newspaper,
> But the driveway was empty,
> And behind the dark trees
> Dawn was turning the sky-vault
> Champagne-shot blue silk,
> A backdrop with roses.

Grosholz is adept at creating a sense of immanence from the ordinary, a discerning eye for what really matters. The title poem 'The Stars of Earth' engages the theme, alluded to above, of getting away from 'electric muses, cell phone, television, texting, Word' and seeing the world as it is outside:

> And as we turned back home, we came to a tree on fire with
>   fireflies,
> A veteran oak encrusted from crown to root with tiny distur-
>   bances
> That pulsed and blazed as if they sang of love, but sang in
>   silence.

That capitalised interjection 'Word' is interestingly sited. It could refer to the word processing program used on computers. Yet it also resonates in popular culture as tag asserting authenticity. In pulling her kids away from their daily distractions, there's a throwback here to theme of the American Renaissance (Emerson, Whitman et al) of the direct encounter with nature, with life instead of filtering it through the screens and barriers created by society. As she puts it in a poem of literary analysis 'The Dream of Chaucer':

> Chaucer seeks rather for the *certeyn thing*
> That in the *Parliament of Fowls* uncovers
> A newfound realism: love and making
> Are things intelligible in their own right
> Apart from sense perception, wish, illusion.

There are a lot of love poems here, both to people and to places, all organised by a lightly worn formalism – her poems are very smooth, flowing – that creates a sense of order that then can be disrupted by a shrewdly chosen word or line break. A small instance in the marriage of style and subject occurs in the homage to her alcoholic travelling salesman father. Describing her father's travels, alone on an evening, the line break is sonically perfect for the dilemma of someone trying to say sober: 'He wants a drink, but holds off for another / Day, another hour.' One drink leads to another unless you don't take that drink: 'The gray Atlantic / Shuffles invisibly. He orders coffee / And maybe calls his sponsor up, long distance.' A quiet drama, but a drama nonetheless played out against the world's indifference.

Grosholz is kind of a throwback in terms of both her style and her sense of poetic vocation i.e. to write about things as she finds them, to constantly be looking for poetic subjects, and to use poetry as a way of interpreting the world. I think of her in terms of someone like Richard Wilbur who died about a year ago. And I suppose Grosholz could be criticised on the same grounds that Wilbur was: that her poems evince a kind of placid, or even elitist, sense of privilege. In both poets there are a fair number of poems about traveling to Italy and other sabbatical spots. There are also engagements with artists and writers, the traditional subject of poetry and also what you might expect from a scholar. And in terms of tone you can say that there is not enough drama or struggle or Big Issues – not enough noise – in them to demand our notice. To which I say, So what? Craftsmanship, even virtuosity, is it's own reward in any artistic performance and Grosholz deserves our attention for the consistently high quality of her writing. And for her insistence that being quiet makes it all the more important that you are heard. Especially these days. Word.

Masterly Control

Chosen Hill, Sue Leigh (Two Rivers) £9.99; *Shrines of Upper Austria*, Phoebe Power (Carcanet) £9.99

Reviewed by JENNIFER EDGECOMBE

'Every century has its tremors', Sue Leigh writes in her debut collection, *Chosen Hill*, and these existential rhythms break out in her poems, as in those to the experimental composers John Cage and Philip Glass – the former captivated with the utilisation of time, having written the world's longest-ever piece of music (lasting hundreds of years), the latter a renowned master of repetition. In the poem 'The artist in old age', Leigh decides that an obsessive Hokusai must have 'understood' the intrinsic relationship between time and nature:

He makes thirty-six views of Fuji.

When he is ninety he thinks
he will understand the mystery.

He will become the mountain.

Leigh takes this idea of complete immersion in the environment a step further in 'Nan Shepherd in the Cairngorms': 'To be with the mountain / as if to know one place / might be enough / for a lifetime'. And still further, in 'Altai burial', the excavated body of a woman who lived in Siberia around 500 BCE is given voice; she has been aware of time passing over her grave, feeling the tremors from 'riders cantering over the / steppe', and a soaking from the 'first hush of snow' that fell and stayed, freezing her remains until the intrusion of the archaeologists.

The word 'snow' or derivatives of it appear seventeen times in *Chosen Hill*, either as an ominous foreshadowing of erasure – during her brother's last days there is a 'sudden late fall of snow' – or continuity: 'Snowflakes / a spring's blossom / the tossed coin of the moon.' For Leigh time is 'a frieze of snow', a beautiful expression which reflects her collection as a whole. Its standout poem is 'Bronze Mirror', about the said object found in a Celtic woman's grave near Birdlip:

You could imagine her
after that long sleep
rising
stretching herself
in the new sunlight
brushing the crumbs of earth
from her hair then

picking it up
to look

In nine short lines, with masterly control, Leigh contracts the span of two thousand years. Reading Leigh's poetry is like 'having faith in a seed' – with repeat reading, each small, ostensibly simple poem grows into something remarkable. They are situated 'between the tidelines', unique and earthly, and offer an answer of sorts – everything we experience is merely the passing of a 'Moment'; 'it is no different / from clouds, trees / a sea of barley / all you are, or might be'.

In another exciting debut, *Shrines of Upper Austria*, Phoebe Power's experiential poems are urgent 'installations' (her word) recording what has been loved or lived: families, politics, traditions – all are finite, death 'nothing more than a great wave' that 'carries us away, at some time or another'. She is present at the shrines, making birth tokens – 'To celebrate the Hanna Lena we cut storks

---

From the Archive

Issue 146, July–August 2002

ALISON BRACKENBURY

From a contribution of nine poems called 'The Hatherley Lane School 1878–2001'. Fellow contributors to this issue include John Ashbery, Caroline Bird, Evelyn Schlag, Edwin Morgan and Chris Wallace-Crabbe.

PROLOGUE

Bell's glint, brick, oak, me. School.
Where did those jackdaws come from
with their black and tumbling wings?

The children? Most sang loud.
Irene, who never could
do sums, was let to run for bread and cheese,

the master's lunch,
up lanes, the tree-hung bridge.
Then children marched away,

lost in a new road's roar,
found lower rooms. I soon lost count
of Irene, whistling by, her head ruffed grey. [...]

/ from hardboard' ('Installation for a New Baby') – or noting the grave goods – 'one unlit red tealight – / two goats died' ('Goat Grave').

Power's poems often have a surreal quality about them. Reality often appears skewed; 'those letterboxes squeezed / to points'. Bells chime wildly – 'tungatungatungatung-atung!' Staccato is deployed – always unpunctuated and often a breathless trio of adjectives ('aqua violet orange' etc). Power is frequently evoking a land beyond this one, the shared experiences more implicit, sensory:

> then they come with lanterns
> pointing orange yellow white
> pointing lantern hats then start to
> multiply in all directions, starshapes,
> lanterns carried everywhere
> bobbing like a lake

There are conversational pieces about Power's Austrian roots, and – through the language of reportage ('they said', 'she said' etc) – human displacement and the Holocaust are sensitively examined at a distance, through a lens of incredulity:

> I only found out about the concentration camps when
> I came to England
>
> in the pubs the gestapo listen and take you away, I thought
>   they take
> you to ordinary prison not the concentration camps where
>   they do
> this and that

When it comes to 'the paragraph on extinction', Power's dry humour successfully and unnervingly captures the fine margin of sublimity in often macabre situations. In an 'Austrian Murder Case':

> The superintendent watched while his men slipped into the water, as easy as steel poles or two long fish. The See closed after their entrance her soft, wide black eyelid.

On a wide array of personal and historical subjects, Power is at heart a storyteller – and a highly readable one. *The Shrines of Upper Austria*, like Sue Leigh's *Chosen Hill*, is an impressive debut.

Gathering Crumbs

Calliope Michail, *Along Mosaic Roads* (The 87 Press) £5

Reviewed by ANTHONY BARNETT

Calliope Michail's *Along Mosaic Roads* is a debut chapbook from The 87 Press. What a wonderful debut it is, both for Michail and for The 87. Michail's background is American and Greek. She grew up in Athens in a house of music: 'the sweet plucking of the / baglama, the rumbling currents of the / cello – I trace my blood'. Currently she lives in London, where she has been studying. She has published translations of the Greek poet Haris Psarras, also UK-based. Described on the cover as 'a series of lyrical peregrinations that chart journeys into the real and imagined spaces of wanderlust, desire, origins and memory' – I can hardly better those words – *Along Mosaic Roads* consists of five sections entitled 'Standing on the Sun'. The opening part-poem of each section is in italic. All except the last section have three more poems, with that central, italic, poem weaving through the whole.

It comes as a shock, on opening the book, to read a second epigraph from Charles Manson. It is not what one would expect. On reflection it is a not uninteresting, not entirely irrelevant, bitter quote (I'll put it that way) more or less about travelling getting one nowhere except where one is. In that, it is a rejoinder to the humane first epigraph from Walt Whitman: 'You road I enter upon and look around, I believe you are not all that is here, I believe that much unseen is also here.' This is true relevance to *Along Mosaic Roads*. In 'Native Stranger': 'I lie barefoot and shrimp eyed / in a city that sleeps with a gaping / mouth of ruins.'

Breathing is the leitmotif in 'Going', in the spacing of the words too: Trees, ocean, desert, clouds, various animals, breathe 'because there is / nothing / / else to do but breathe'. 'Carte de Tendre' opens 'You don't know what love is, / you sang to me, our legs pretzeled at the end / of the bed, so I did my research and decided / to make myself / a map –'. Michail does know what love is. Her poems are love poems to people and places. 'Gathering Crumbs', for Grandma Estela: 'She gathers the crumbs / on the kitchen table, handmade mosaic / a geologist's tender fancy –'.

In 'Native Stranger', voices intersect:

>   speaking a language I can
>   understand, a language rooted
>   in the land, tightly woven through my
>   spine, a language I can use, a language
> I can't curse in   a language
> I don't dream in.

I cannot say exactly where Michail has found her poetry but I think it shares with some Greek poets, Elytis comes to mind, a concretised nostalgia, not for the past but for the present–future. Calliope: beautiful-voiced muse of poetry and song. How was it known, in her naming, in the imagining, that Calliope Michail would become that for real? On a pedestal? Yes, I do place *Along Mosaic Roads* on a pedestal, so to speak. Though not one that is fixed. One that is moving, towards roads to come. In 'X', 'I dance I / dance with paint on my soles.'

Canadian Poet

Nancy Mattson, *Vision on Platform 2* (Shoestring Press) £10

Reviewed by LEAH FRITZ

The first part of *Vision on Platform 2* is devoted to Nancy Mattson's childhood in the countryside of Western Canada. What it was like to be there and what it was like to move, or have to move, to London is important to the poet's life, and the negatives are presented in the first part of this collection. She objects to a house called '5212': 'I wish it could be Cherryville Cottage, but no / I'd have to name it Chokecherry House':

My elementary fingers trace letters,
birth and death numbers,
sharp cuts into smooth slabs...

These memories wind up with 'I can subtract in my head.', an index to her age at the time this happened. In 'Widow, Marooned' she tells how a flood sent them away: 'I am thirsty / for the dustbowl of my youth.'

Here Mattson is singing. She sometimes tries not to, but much of the poetry gets there, anyhow. She quotes Anna Akhmatova, and then writes about her death:

Bury your fear that she was lost in a field
Trust foxes and deer to visit her grave
Assume that nettles and thistles adorn it
   and that snow and wind sing antiphons.

There is something of a suggestion here that Mattson holds tightly to her Christian beliefs. This is followed by a poem called 'Threads for a Woman Priest'. Mattson is also a feminist, and this poem, in turn, is followed by one called 'Miracle in Essex Road' (London) in which the author quotes a woman pushing a baby carriage. '*Six months and I'm lucky to have him. We both / nearly died at his birth when my heart gave out.*' Mattson then cannot recall if the woman mentioned her son's name, but she, herself, says her own daughter's. (Well, there are moments in this book when Mattson tugs at your heartstrings. Why not?)

Quoting women poets at the head of each chapter, a number of her own poems are ekphrastic, as well. The title poem begins:

I didn't realise I was reading
Seamus Heaney's poem in *Seeing Things*
on the very day the Irish honour the holy
St. Patrick. Let me assure you, he has no role
in this tale [...]

And later: 'They didn't know/ that a Hackney cousin of Robert Doisneau / had captured them forever on his smartphone, // silent, upon a bench at 'Seven Sisters'.

The joke is that seven nuns turned up at Seven Sisters station on the tube. In the last stanza, Nancy Mattson writes:

I was there that morning and I swear
that only and exactly seven sisters sat
beneath that sign, a sevenfold blessing.
Let no one mock this miracle of symmetry.
Let no one credit photoshop, St. Patrick
or the inspiration of Seamus Heaney's
'squaring, crossings, lightenings or settings.'

Nancy Mattson's *Vision on Platform 2* is both a brilliant collection of poems and a sack of schmaltz. I loved it – all!

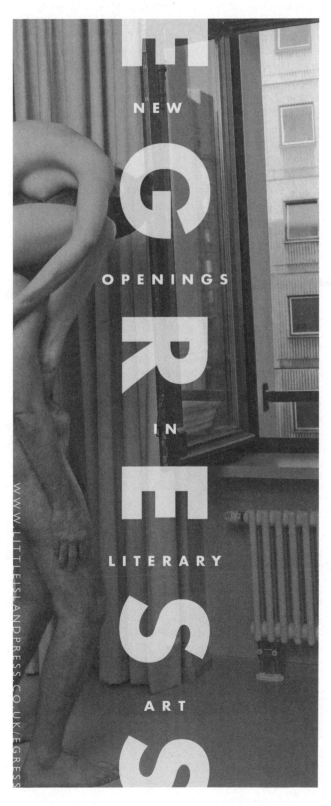

Lynette Thorstensen is a New Zealander who has lived for ten years in the Auvergne, France. Her poetry has been published in *Landfall* and *takahē* magazines in New Zealand and *Southerly* magazine in Australia. **Maitreya-bandhu**'s debut collection, *The Crumb Road* (Bloodaxe, 2013) is a PBS Recommendation. *Yarn*, also with Bloodaxe, was published in 2015. His book-length sequence, *After Cézanne*, is forthcoming. **Margo Berdeshevsky**'s newest collection is *Before The Drought*, (Glass Lyre Press,) finalist for the National Poetry Series. Author as well of *Between Soul & Stone*, and *But a Passage in Wilderness*, (Sheep Meadow Press,) and *Beautiful Soon Enough*, (Fiction Collective Two/ University of Alabama Press.) NYC born, she lives in Paris. **William Poulos** is a poet and commentator. Among his other projects, he is researching Alexander Pope's engagement with Latin poetry. **Beau Hopkins** was born in 1982 and grew up in in Oxfordshire. He studied for a BA in French and Spanish at Oxford University, and an MA in Creative Writing at the University of East Anglia. He has lived and worked in Spain, France and Uganda, where in 2012 the production of his play, *The River and the Mountain*, attracted global attention and was censored by the Ugandan Media Council. His début poetry pamphlet, *Figment Music*, a sequence of nineteen experimental sonnets, was published by Gatehouse Press in 2017. He is currently working on his first full-length collection of poems, which will include free contemporary translations of the Vulgate psalms, Ovid's exile poems and the Acoli-language song poems of Ugandan poet Okot p'Bitek. He is finishing a PhD in Creative and Critical Writing at the University of East Anglia, for which he has written a thesis on J.H. Prynne's 2011 volume, *Kazoo Dreamboats*. **Angela Leighton**'s most recent poetry publications are *Spills* (Carcanet, 2016), and *Five Poems* (Clutag Press, 2018). **Jena Schmitt** lives in Sault Ste. Marie, Ontario, Canada, with her family. **Art Beck** is a San Francisco poet, essayist and poetry translator. His *Mea Roma, a Meditative Sampling from M. Valerius Martia-* lis (2018) was published by Shearsman. **Jamie Osborn** is a poet, translator and activist, now in Norwich. His work is featured in Carcanet's *New Poetries VII* and in February he read his co-translations from modern Assyrian at the British Museum. **Joe Carrick-Varty** won the 2017/18 New Poets Prize and his debut pamphlet *Somewhere Far* is forthcoming with The Poetry Business in June 2019. **Jennifer Edgecombe** lives on the Kent coast. Her poems and reviews have appeared in *Ambit, Caught By the River, Lighthouse* and elsewhere. **N. S. Thompson** is the non-fiction editor of Able Muse. He co-edited *A Modern Don Juan: Cantos for these Times* (2014) and his most recent poetry collection is *Mr Larkin on Photography and Other Poems* (2016). **Jennie Feldman** has published two collections of poems, *The Lost Notebook* and *Swift* (Anvil/Carcanet). She has just completed a third. **Carol Rumens**'s pamphlet, *Bezdelki/Small Things* (The Emma Press), with illustrations by Emma Wright, won the Michael Marks Award for Best Poetry Pamphlet, 2018. **Stewart Sanderson** is a poet from Glasgow. He was recently awarded the 2019 Jessie Kesson Fellowship at Moniack Mhor. His second pamphlet, *An Offering*, was published last year by Tapsalteerie. **Leah Fritz** has written five collections of poetry. A few of her reviews and poems have been published in *PNR*. **James Tate**'s awards included the Pulitzer Prize, the Academy of American Poets Wallace Stevens Award and the National Book Award. Tate's latest collection, *The Government Lake*, is published by Ecco HarperCollins (July 2019). **Sheri Benning**'s third collection of poetry, *The Season's Vagrant Light: New and Selected Poems*, was published by Carcanet Press in 2015. She's published two books in Canada: *Thin Moon Psalm* (Brick Books) and *Earth After Rain* (Thistledown Press). She is currently a lecturer in creative writing at the University of Saskatchewan. **André Naffis-Sahely** is the author of *The Promised Land: Poems from Itinerant Life* (Penguin, 2017). His translations include over twenty titles of poetry, fiction and nonfiction. He is the poetry editor of *Ambit* magazine.

COLOPHON

Editors
Michael Schmidt
Andrew Latimer

Editorial address
The Editors at the address on the right. Manuscripts cannot be returned unless accompanied by a stamped addressed envelope or international reply coupon.

Trade distributors
NBN International
10 Thornbury Road
Plymouth PL6 7PP, UK
orders@nbninternational.com

Design
Typeset by Andrew Latimer
in Arnhem Pro

Represented by
Compass IPS Ltd
Great West House
Great West Road, Brentford
TW8 9DF, UK
sales@compass-ips.london

Copyright
© 2019 Poetry Nation Review
All rights reserved
ISBN 978-1-78410-157-2
ISSN 0144-7076

Subscriptions (6 issues)
INDIVIDUALS (print and digital):
£39.50; abroad £49
INSTITUTIONS (print only): £76;
abroad £90
INSTITUTIONS (digital):
subscriptions from Exact Editions
(https://shop.exacteditions.com/
gb/pn-review)
to: *PN Review*, Alliance House,
30 Cross Street, Manchester
M2 7AQ, UK

Supported by

Supported using public funding by
ARTS COUNCIL ENGLAND